# Foundations in Singing

SEVENTH EDITION

# Foundations in Singing

*A Basic Textbook in Vocal Technique and Song Interpretation*

## John Glenn Paton

*Professor of Voice Emeritus*
*University of Colorado, Boulder*

## Van A. Christy *(deceased)*

*Professor Emeritus*
*University of California, Santa Barbara*

Boston   Burr Ridge, IL   Dubuque, IA   Madison, WI   New York   San Francisco   St. Louis
Bangkok   Bogotá   Caracas   Kuala Lumpur   Lisbon   London   Madrid   Mexico City
Milan   Montreal   New Delhi   Santiago   Seoul   Singapore   Sydney   Taipei   Toronto

# McGraw-Hill Higher Education ⚡

*A Division of The* **McGraw-Hill** *Companies*

Foundations in Singing, Seventh Edition
A Basic Textbook in Vocal Technique and Song Interpretation

Published by McGraw-Hill, an imprint of The McGraw-Hill Companies, Inc., 1221 Avenue of the Americas, New York, NY 10020. Copyright © 2002, 1997 by The McGraw-Hill Companies, Inc. All rights reserved. No part of this publication may be reproduced or distributed in any form or by any means, or stored in a data base or retrieval system, without the prior written consent of The McGraw-Hill Companies, Inc., including, but not limited to, in any network or other electronic storage or transmission, or broadcast for distance learning.

Some ancillaries, including electronic and print components, may not be available to customers outside the United States.

This book is printed on acid-free paper.

3 4 5 6 7 8 9 0 QPD/QPD 0 9 8 7 6 5 4 3

ISBN 0-07-241425-1

Publisher: *Phillip A. Butcher*
Executive sponsoring editor: *Christopher Freitag*
Developmental editor: *Elsa Peterson*
Marketing manager: *David Patterson*
Project editor: *Anna M. Chan*
Production supervisor: *Susanne Riedell*
Media producer: *Gregg Di Lorenzo*
Designer: *Mary Kazak*
Cover illustration: *Andy Powell*
Supplement producer: *Erin Sauder*
Typeface: *10/12 Palatino*
Compositor: *A-R Editions, Inc.*
Printer: *Quebecor World Dubuque Inc.*

Library of Congress Cataloging-in-Publication Data

Christy, Van Ambrose, 1900–
    Foundations in singing : a basic textbook in vocal technique and song interpretation /
Van A. Christy, John Glenn Paton. — 7th ed.
      p. cm.
    Includes indexes.
    ISBN 0-07-241425-1 (alk. paper)
    1. Singing—Methods. 2. Songs—Interpretation (Phrasing, dynamics, etc.) I. Paton, John
Glenn. II. Title.
MT825 .C52 2002
783'.04—dc21
                                 2001031684

www.mhhe.com

# Contents

# Song Contents

**Musical Theater Songs and Popular Song Classics (Listed chronologically)**

*These songs are located out of chronological order so as to avoid awkward page turns in the surrounding songs.

# Preface

A whole generation of singers has found a solid "foundation in singing" in this book. Originated by the late Dr. Van A. Christy, the first editions of *Foundations in Singing* distilled a store of practical wisdom from his *Expressive Singing*. Six separate editions have kept the book in touch with current discoveries in vocal science and current musical taste. In the seventh edition the focus remains as it has always been: to introduce new singers to the time-honored techniques of classical singing and vocal performance.

*Foundations in Singing* serves the needs of voice students in their first full year of study, whether in high school or college, whether in private lessons or in group or class instruction. By assigning readings in the textbook, the teacher saves instruction time and ensures that the student learns essential vocabulary and concepts. Easy, safe vocal exercises ensure that basics are covered, and they are given simple harmonizations so that they are musical experiences, even at an early level. The teacher has plenty of scope to add other exercises, and the book's positive language affirms and reinforces the teacher's indispensable role.

This new edition offers many improvements:

- The text has been thoughtfully revised for more logical flow;
- Basic principles are summarized at the end of each chapter in a few statements that begin with "Always . . .";
- The page count has increased;
- The total number of songs has risen to 65, and 12 of these are printed in two keys, high and low;
- Sight-singing exercises are included in chapter 12 for the first time;
- Recorded accompaniments are now available on compact discs. While it is still ideal to have an expert accompanist in the classroom, CDs offer an economical tool for students to learn songs with strong instrumental support.

*Foundations in Singing* provides a systematic approach to vocal technique that has been validated by years of experience: attitude, posture, breathing, tone and resonance, song preparation, English diction, performance, and extending the voice. Two additional chapters on vocal physiology and music fundamentals may be used flexibly or assigned for outside reading, as students need them.

Ten unison songs and four rounds are included here because of their usefulness for energizing a class, warming up voices, and introducing musical and vocal fundamentals.

The anthology of solo songs includes an international selection of 10 songs from folk traditions, 24 accessible classics from four centuries, and 17 selections from musicals from 1930 to the 1990s. All songs have been thoroughly reviewed, and primary sources from the seventeenth to the twentieth centuries have been used whenever possible.

Several foreign languages are included for students who want to use their favorite language in a song. Every foreign text is translated literally on the music page where the text first appears; this translation follows normal English word order and can be extracted for use in program notes.

Appendix A, *Notes on the Songs*, goes beyond what students can normally research on their own. Background knowledge awakens students' interest and helps them relate their songs to other disciplines. The notes include interpretations of moods, unusual words in the poems, and musical sources. Foreign texts are translated, and IPA transcriptions are given.

Appendix B presents the complete International Phonetic Alphabet (IPA) for English and other languages.

## Acknowledgments

Writing a book for beginning singers calls on resources and experience from throughout my entire life. Above all, the students who worked with me in the past 40 years have shown me what works and doesn't work in vocal pedagogy, and I am grateful for their patience with me.

Aside from the teachers mentioned in my biography, I have learned and been influenced by many others, including Laura May Titus, Dr. R. Berton Coffin, Oren Brown, Jon Peck, Mario Carta, and Jo Estill. All singers are indebted to the National Association of Teachers of Singing for fostering an exchange of knowledge such as no one imagined a generation ago.

Thanks to Dr. Warren Hoffer, who first recommended me for this enjoyable project. Helpful and specific comments about this edition have been contributed by Paul Berkolds, Carol Clary-Weber, Julie Fortney, Cheryl Roach, James Stemen, William Trabold, and Garnet Tree. Janice McVeigh gave me the idea of the "Always . . ." statements. Elisabeth Howard suggested effective Broadway selections. Dr. René Aravena corrected the phonetic transcriptions of Spanish songs. My editor, Elsa Peterson, made many practical suggestions, and some of her words found their way into the text.

Valuable suggestions came from my professional peers who reviewed the text of the previous edition, including: Dr. Phillip C. Collister, Towson University; Nancy Jo Davidson, Skidmore College; Dr. Helen Dilworth, City College San Francisco; Kathleen Hacker, University of Indianapolis; Flora Y. Martin, Prince George's Community College; Melanie Mitrano, New Jersey City University; Blanche Schultz, Chicago State University; Carole J. Seitz, Creighton University; Kelly Ann Westover, Irvine Valley College.

Thanks and love go to my wife, Joan Thompson, who supports my research and writing in every possible way and makes my books better by her perceptive comments.

With the publication of *Foundations in Singing*, plans for its next revised edition will begin immediately. Readers and users of the book are sincerely invited to send comments and suggestions to me in care of the publisher, so that the next edition can be made even better.

John Glenn Paton
Los Angeles, California
Professor of Voice Emeritus, University of Colorado at Boulder
Lecturer, University of Southern California

**About the Author**

John Glenn Paton grew up in a musical home in New Castle, Pennsylvania. He studied at the Cincinnati Conservatory of Music under Franklin Bens and Sonia Essin. After military service he studied further at the Eastman School of Music under Julius Huehn. Through both Essin and Huehn he traces his vocal lineage to Anna Schoen-René and through her to Pauline Viardot-Garcia.

After studying lieder interpretation in Stuttgart, Germany, under composer Hermann Reutter, he began to teach at the University of Wisconsin and also sang annual concert tours with Reutter as his accompanist. After moving to the University of Colorado at Boulder, he received a fellowship to conduct a semester of research in Rome, Italy.

Living in California since 1986, Paton taught class voice to acting students at the American Academy of Dramatic Arts, Pasadena. In 1989 he joined the faculty of the University of Southern California. He celebrated his 60th birthday by giving a solo recital, and he continues to perform occasionally.

Building on the work of the original author, Dr. Van A. Christy, who died in 1990, Paton extensively revised the fifth and sixth editions of *Foundations in Singing*. He also made instructional editions of vocal music for G. Schirmer, Leyerle Publications, and Alfred Publishing Co. His books are found in voice studios around the world, and he teaches master classes in diction and song interpretation.

# 1 | Freedom to Sing

*Guiding Questions:*

*Can I learn to sing better than I already do?*
*What should I expect from voice classes or from private lessons?*
*What do I need? How do I get started?*

EVERYONE has an urge to sing—it's built into us! Singing is part of every human community on the earth. Singing brings us together in shared group feelings, helping us interact, work, and play together. A person who sings is telling a story to the listeners, whether the song is a lullaby, play song, love song, or hymn— there is no limit on what songs can be sung.

## Can I learn to sing?

Emphatically: "Yes!" Anyone who has a normal speaking voice and can "carry a tune" (or can learn to do so) can learn to sing well, with confidence and pleasure.

Your singing voice is a potential musical instrument, waiting for you to learn how to use it. Most people don't realize that singing can be practiced and learned.

In fact, singing is a skill that you can learn if you have a capable teacher and willingness to practice regularly over a period of time. Yes, talent plays a role, but with study and practice your voice will improve in ways that you cannot foresee when you start out.

### Singing with confidence

You may be one of the many persons who have a "fear of singing." Let's look at some of the reasons for such a fear.

Singing begins with hearing musical tones with the ear, imagining tones in the brain, and forming them with the muscles of the throat. This coordination, ear-brain-throat, is natural but complex. A few children can sing reliably in tune at an early age, but most cannot yet do so when they begin school. If a child does not hear singing at home or have a teacher skilled in music at school, early attempts at singing may be discouraging. Many adults sadly remember that they were labeled as non-singers or were ridiculed because they sang out of tune as children.

Some boys and girls enjoy singing in grade school but stop singing during puberty because they feel insecure with the new physical sensations that go along with having an adult larynx. They stay silent or perhaps they sing along with the radio when they are alone. They do not know that with a bit of courage and a short course of instruction they can start to have fun singing with others and for others.

If you are one of the lucky ones, you have learned the fun of singing at home, at school, in church or around a campfire. You know the satisfaction of letting out your feelings in songs. You have a basis of confidence from which you can begin immediately to improve your singing and increase your knowledge about your

1

voice. As you progress, remember to encourage others along the way; never cut down anyone who sincerely tries to sing well.

## How will I improve my singing?

Imagination—your ability to imagine a singing tone—is the chief means of control you have over your singing voice. The sound that you hear in your imagination is like a message to your muscles, and they do their best to produce the sound that you are imagining.

That is why learning to sing is a double process: It includes mental concepts and good muscular habits. You already have certain vocal abilities, including the way you speak and sing. As you better understand how your voice works, you will use daily practice to form better vocal habits and eliminate habits that are causing trouble. With a positive, enthusiastic approach toward singing, you yourself are the most important factor in the learning process.

The next most important factor is your teacher, who cares about helping you to sing better and has the skill and experience to do so. Your teacher will show you new ways to sing and set up step-by-step goals that allow you to experience success and growing confidence. (If you want to know about your teacher's training and musical career, it's OK to ask.)

The most basic process in voice instruction is that your teacher will *listen to you and suggest how to sing better.* This process may start at your first meeting, either with a song that you have prepared or with unrehearsed singing of a simple song like "America." Perhaps you will do some easy vocal exercises. After you have taken this first plunge, the teacher will offer you some new ideas by demonstrating and explaining them. You will be assigned readings in this book to reinforce them. All through your lessons, the teacher will listen for the best sounds that you can make, because it is important to notice what techniques work best for you and to use them more and more.

## Private lessons or classes?

If you are taking private voice lessons, you have two main advantages:

- Your teacher's full attention for the length of the lesson; and
- The privilege of moving ahead at your own pace.

If you are receiving instruction in a small group or in a voice class, you have other advantages:

- You will gain confidence from seeing that other people have difficulties like your own;
- You can try out new techniques in the safety of group singing;
- You will see the techniques that help other students improve;
- You will understand new concepts better through questions and discussions with your peers;
- You will lose your qualms about singing in front of others, as others encourage you and you encourage them.

In either private or group lessons you have responsibilities. If you are going to miss a private lesson, the teacher needs to know at least a day ahead in order to give your lesson time to someone else. If you arrive late or miss a lesson without advance notice, it is time lost, and you cannot expect the teacher to make it up.

If you are in a voice class, remember that you are a participating individual, not just a seat number in a lecture hall. If you arrive late or leave early, it disrupts the work that others are doing. If you miss class, the process goes on for others without you.

Between meetings with your teacher, practice singing daily. As with sports and other physical skills, you cannot "cram" the experience of vocal growth by extra practicing before an exam. There is also mental work to do: Read the assigned text and work on learning your songs. Learn more about singing by hearing recordings and live musical performances.

## Shall I sing in a choral organization?

Yes, definitely (unless your teacher advises against it!). Look for a chorus with good leadership, with a leader who teaches good vocal habits in the rehearsals and challenges you with music that stretches your potential. A good conductor will teach you to listen more keenly and sing better in tune, so that your music-reading skills will improve along with your vocal technique. You will be singing alongside others who also love to sing, and you will learn from each other.

If a choir does not serve your needs, look for a better one. If time is wasted from poor organization or poor discipline, if the music is not exciting to sing, or if your throat hurts from poor rehearsal methods, go elsewhere. There are many choruses and choirs; you just have to look for the right one.

## What will I need?

This book provides enough practice material and songs for your first year of vocal study. With the book are two CDs containing piano accompaniments of all the songs.

You also need a solitary, quiet place where you can sing our freely without worrying about other people. A living room with family members around is not the right place, nor is a thin-walled apartment with neighbors at home. A practice room in a music school is ideal. Alternatively, you might be able to rent a space at a local church, or ask your teacher for other ideas. A mirror in your practice room will be useful to check your posture and appearance while singing.

You also need some way to produce specific pitches, at best a piano or other musical instrument. A pitch pipe, available at any music store, will do, and it can be carried wherever you go. Or you can record the pitches you need on a recorder.

In addition to playing the accompaniment CDs, you need to be able to record yourself during your lessons or classes as well as outside them. You need both a CD player and a cassette recorder, or else one device that does both jobs. With your teacher's permission, use your recorder in every class. When you sing the first few times, you may be too nervous or excited to remember how well you performed. Your recorder will let you hear again what comments were made and how your singing improved subsequently. A portable cassette recorder does not reproduce your voice quality perfectly, but even a poor quality recording will tell you honestly whether you are singing on time and in tune.

## Physical freedom

Singing feels good physically, provided that your body is healthy and that you sing correctly and freely. When your singing feels natural and easy, your imagination is activating many sets of muscles, some of them very tiny and most of them out of sight. That is why we achieve more with mental concentration than by direct muscular control.

The physical work of singing happens this way: The brain imagines a desired sound. Nerves carry messages in the form of electrical charges to the muscles that need to work. The muscles contract as little or as much as they need to, becoming shorter and thicker. When finished working, they relax and become longer again.

**How interference occurs**

Freedom in singing requires that the muscles that are active in singing can do their work without interference from other muscles. Such interference—we call it "tension"—comes from various causes.

When a muscle finishes working, it may fail to relax completely. Some muscle fibers remain tense, leaving the muscle partially contracted. Sore shoulders after driving or carrying a load of books are a familiar example of this kind of residual tension. Singing goes better if you get rid of such tensions first.

When a muscle is active, there may also be partial activation of a nearby muscle because connections exist between neighboring nerves. This is a second cause of unnecessary tension. For instance, many of us have slight tensions in our speaking habits because the tiny muscles involved are so close to each other.

A third source of unwanted tension is that the nervous system sends out signals to the muscles even during rest, testing periodically to assure that the pathways for nerve impulses are open. These signals cause slight contractions of the muscles. This is why our long muscles grow shorter during sleep and it feels good to stretch them when we awaken.

**Stretching**

A good way to dispel unwanted tension in a muscle is by stretching it. Gentle, patient stretching allows time for the muscle fibers to reach their maximum length. When a stretch is released, the muscle returns to a neutral, relaxed position. Three pieces of advice go with every stretching exercise:

- If any exercise causes pain, stop it immediately;
- Breathe in and out normally, without holding your breath;
- A stretched muscle is in a weak position; do not shock it by a bouncing movement.

Massage is another way of helping muscles to give up unwanted tension.

**Discomfort? Stop!**

Suppose that you are in good health but that singing causes you some physical discomfort or even pain. In this case, the active muscles are receiving interference from other muscles, causing them to overwork.

If this happens, you should stop singing and rest for at least 30 seconds while you think about what you have been doing and how to make a change for the better. The cause may be physical: You may need to stretch, to take a better breath, or to sing for awhile in a different part of your range. Or your brain may be sending unclear messages to your voice, so that the muscles were responding in a confused way. This happens easily when we are trying something new. The remedy is to clarify your mental image of the sound, word and pitch you want to produce.

**Getting started**

Starting now, you will exercise your voice daily. Make it part of your schedule five or six days a week. (One day a week of voice rest is a good idea.) For most people it works well to practice for short periods of 10–20 minutes in a concentrated way. If these short periods add up to an hour of thoughtful practice a day, you will make steady progress.

Just as in sports training, vocal practice begins with a warmup that consists of easy exercises. Some objectives:

- To prepare your mind and body for singing;
- To energize your breathing;
- To explore parts of your voice that are not used in daily speech until your voice is working easily through most of its range.

# Exercises

It is worthwhile to begin your practice period with a minute or two of stretching. Since you probably have favorite stretches already (and your teacher can show you more), I'll give you just one of my favorites now.

**1.1** **Rib Stretch.** Stand straight, with your weight on the left foot. Bend your right knee so as to lower your right hip. Reach up with your right arm and stretch toward the ceiling. While continuing to stretch, move your arm forward and back slowly for 10–15 seconds. Relax, then repeat on the other side. Repeat on both sides. Purpose: to stretch the small muscles between your ribs, the intercostals, so that you can use full lung capacity when you want to.

The next exercises energize your breath. (The next chapter tells more about the breath, but these exercises are to get you started.)

**1.2** **SH.** Say "sh" and prolong the sound for 3–5 seconds. Round your lips so that the sound is not harsh. Feel that your abdominal muscles contract gently, pushing the air out. Then relax the abdominals and let air come back into your body effortlessly. Repeat several times. Purpose: to begin using breath in an intentional way, rather than as an unconscious reflex.

**1.3** **Breath Pulses.** Say "sh-sh-sh-sh-sh," as a continuous sound but with pulses produced by gentle action of your abdominal muscles. Relax and let air come back into your body effortlessly. Repeat several times. Purpose: the same as ex. 1.2.

Songs require a wider range of tones, highs and lows, than most people use in daily conversation. But we all have these high and low tones and probably use them when we are excited. Let's explore them in the speaking voice before trying to sing them.

**1.4** **Hum Slide.** Speak an "m" on a downward slide, starting a little higher than you normally speak. Use an expression of pleasant curiosity, as if you are encouraging someone else to speak. As you repeat this several times, let the voice start on higher and higher pitches, as long as they are comfortable. It is not important exactly what pitches you use. Try low pitches too. Purpose: to explore the whole pitch range that you can use with comfort.

**1.5** **Happy Talk.** Say "Hi" in an excited, surprised voice. Start on a higher pitch level than you usually use, and then let your voice slide down to a normal pitch. Repeat several times, starting a little higher each time. Allow your voice to go high, but don't push—this is not a competition. Do the same with other exclamations, such as:
"Hey!," "Who?," "Wow!," and "Whee!."
Keep up your enthusiasm, an important ingredient in the exercise. Purpose: to wake up the full range of the speaking voice in a natural way.

A major goal of voice training is to equalize the higher and lower tones, making them as consistent with each other and as easy as possible. Singing "slides" helps toward this goal by allowing the voice to make easy, smooth adjustments between higher and lower tones. When the tones are easy and consistent, a slide will no longer be necessary.

The next exercise uses the musical interval of a 5th, which is the distance between the first and fifth notes of a scale. You can imagine a 5th downward by mentally singing the first three notes of "The Star-Spangled Banner"; the distance between the first and third notes is a 5th.

**1.6** **Hum Slide 5th.** Hum any pitch and slide down a 5th. (You may think "Oh, say!" while you hum in order to get the interval right.) Slide down-up-down-up-down, starting on the upper note and ending on the lower one.

Repeat in various parts of your range, changing higher and lower. Purpose: to explore your comfortable singing range with more control of pitch.

CD 1 Track 2

1.7   **Oo Slide 5th.** Sing "Who" softly, using the same pattern as in "Hum Slide 5th." Also try the syllables "You" and "Loo." Purpose: to explore your comfortable range with a quiet singing tone.

ALWAYS Concentrate 100% when practicing.
   (To sing while washing dishes or driving your car is fun, but it is not practicing.)

ALWAYS Sing with a positive expectation.
   (Your singing is going to be good, and it is going to get better.)

ALWAYS Encourage other singers in their singing.
   (Never discourage anyone from singing.)

# 2 Breath and the Body

**Guiding Questions:** *How should I sit or stand to sing?*
*How do singers breathe?*

DOES just hearing the word "posture" make you stiffen up? Good posture for singing is definitely not stiff. Good posture has two aspects: having the body ready for action, and how the body is used during the action. If the body is out of line or off balance, then muscles have to work to keep it erect; if the muscles are stiff, then every action has to overcome that stiffness.

## Singing posture

Good posture for singing means using the body in such a way that our breathing muscles work easily and there is no interference to the sound we want to produce. Poor posture may mean that your lungs cannot expand fully or that your voice cannot reach all of the notes you should be able to sing because the throat is stretched out of its proper shape.

Experienced performers can sing in almost any position, even lying down. Musical theater performers must be able to sing while dancing, and in most Asian countries singers sit down to perform. But while we are discovering and freeing our voices, an erect, standing posture gives us the best start.

## Body alignment

Here's what to do:

**Figure 2.1**

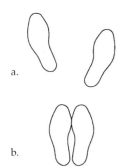

- Feet: Let your heels be a few inches apart, with the toes turned out slightly and one foot a little forward. Keep both feet on the floor. With your feet in the position of figure 2.1a, you stand firmly, but you can shift your weight in any direction. With the position in Figure 2.1b, your posture looks stiff, and you may wobble or weave around.
- Legs: Straight, but not rigid or locked at the knees.
- Torso: Keep your hips and shoulders level. Your back muscles hold the torso erect so that the abdominal muscles can play their important role in giving you flexible breath control.
- Shoulders: Let them relax downward and back. If your shoulders hunch up out of fear or insecurity, the tension may carry over into your singing. Relaxing your shoulders makes you feel and look more confident. But relaxation is not slouching—if the shoulders are slouched forward, your lungs cannot expand properly.

- Neck and head: Let them rise effortlessly toward the ceiling. Imagine that a puppeteer is lifting you from above by a string that pulls up on your head, directly over and between your ears. Let your head remain level so that your eyes look straight ahead, neither down nor up, as in figure 2.2a.

**Head alignment**

The weight of your head—an average person's head weighs about 11 pounds—is meant to be balanced on the topmost vertebra of your spinal column, located midway between your ears. If your posture is lazy, as in figure 2.2b, the neck and shoulder muscles have to work constantly to keep your head from falling forward. Their tension can spread to other muscles and interfere with singing.

A slouched posture also stretches the muscles at the front of the neck somewhat, and they become less free to do what we want.

Avoid stretching your neck upward, as in figure 2.2c, to reach for high notes. Children do so because their soft voice boxes need the pull of external muscles, but adults do not need to stretch their necks.

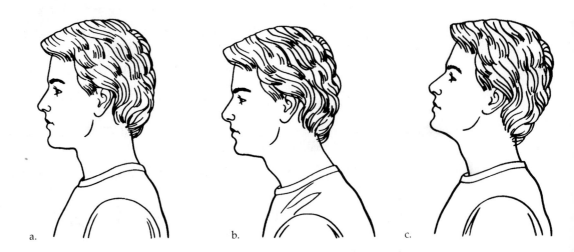

**Figure 2.2**

# Breathing well to sing well

We have all been breathing at about 16 times per minute all our lives, breathing faster when we exercise, and using our breath to speak and shout all we want. Even so, singing makes special demands on our breath:

- Singing long musical phrases depends on both the volume of air in our lungs and on our ability to release air slowly and steadily;
- Singing louder and softer and singing with expression and variety depend on our ability to vary the rate of airflow;
- Musical rhythm often requires us to breathe in quickly between phrases.

Here are our objectives in learning to breathe well for singing:

- To release breath energy at a precisely controlled rate and degree of pressure;
- To maintain a free flow for a desired length of time;
- To transform the breath into tone without wasting any; and
- To renew the energy quickly by taking a new breath.

These objectives sum up what singers mean by **breath control.** If "control" has a negative meaning for you, perhaps a more positive phrase is **breath management.**

**The breathing mechanism**

The way singers use their breath may seem mysterious because it involves various groups of interactive muscles that are all out of sight. We will try to learn about them in the simplest way possible, through using and feeling them in action. After we do a couple of experiments and think about them, we will better understand **breath support.**

First, see how much air you can push out of your body. Squeeze your ribs in on both sides, using your elbows to help. Pull in your abdominal muscles at the same time. After holding this position for three or four seconds, relax, let air back into your lungs, and then think about what has just happened.

Here are some questions about what you just did. Does your experience agree with the answers suggested? If not, try again.

Q. Could you push *all* of the air out of your body?

A. No, there is always some air left in the lungs, residual air. You are never completely out of air, but you can reach a point where it is uncomfortable to push more air out.

Q. If you tried to keep the air out of your body for more than a minute, what would happen? Would you faint?

A. The body would relax involuntarily and air would rush in; you would not faint.

Q. When you decided to breathe again, was it hard to get air or did it come in automatically? Does this tell you anything about singing?

A. Air rushed in automatically. While singing, you can take air in very quickly, just by making space for the air to rush into.

Before going on to the next experiment, let's take notice of some facts about anatomy.

You know that air is stored in the two lungs. You may not know that the lungs are merely sacks, subdivided into thousands of tiny sub-compartments. They have no muscles of their own; rather, they adhere to the ribs, growing smaller when the ribs move in and larger when they move out.

You used a number of different muscles, but there are two principal muscle groups that help you to push air out of the body:

1. Muscles that pull the ribs down, called **internal intercostal muscles,** which translates in simple English to "inside, between-the-ribs muscles." These short muscles connect each rib to the one below it. Working on both sides of your body, they pull diagonally down and back, toward the lower part of the spine;

2. The **abdominal muscles,** which pull in your tummy and keep it from bulging out because of the pressure caused by the internal intercostal muscles. There are three layers of abdominal muscles with fibers running in different directions, but we are only interested in the way they act together to tighten your tummy and push air out.

Here is the second experiment:

Try to widen your rib cage from side to side. Either hold your hands to your sides and push outward against them, or push out against a partner's hands, as in figure 2.3.

At the same time, relax your abdominal muscles so that your tummy wall moves gently outward, opening up space so that air rushes into your lungs. Again, a partner can help, as shown in figure 2.4, by checking whether the outward movement is really taking place.

After holding this position for three or four seconds, let your abdominal muscles pull in again, pushing the breath out, while the ribs return to their relaxed position. You may need to repeat this several times to open up your chest cavity fully. Then relax and think about what just happened.

Figure 2.3

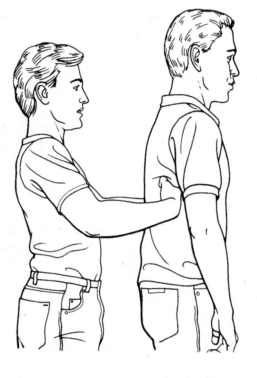

Figure 2.4

Here are some questions about what you just did. Does your experience agree with the answers suggested? If not, try again.

Q. With a widened rib cage, could you take in more air than you expected?

A. Probably. Even if the abdominal muscles work perfectly, your lungs cannot reach maximum capacity if the chest is collapsed.

Q. What happened when the abdominal muscles relaxed?

A. The abdominal organs moved down and outward, helped by gravity. The lungs then could expand lower, letting more air in.

Q. Could the same action occur if you were lying down and gravity did not help? Are muscles also doing part of the work?

A. Yes to both questions. The main muscle that is helping is inside and out of sight.

Let's notice some more facts about anatomy.

All twelve ribs on each side are connected to spinal vertebrae in back. The seven highest pairs of ribs are also attached to the breastbone (sternum) through cartilages that allow them a small range of motion. The next three pairs can move much more because they are not attached directly to the breastbone; rather, each rib is attached through cartilage to the rib above. The two lowest pairs are attached only to the spine.

In this experiment you used a number of different muscles, but there are two principal muscle groups that help to pull air into the body:

1. Muscles that lift the ribs, called **external intercostal muscles,** "outside, between-the-ribs muscles." These short muscles connect each rib to the one below it. On both sides of your body they pull diagonally upward and back, toward the upper part of the spine. These are the muscles, principally in the back, that you used to widen your ribs.

2. The **diaphragm** (Greek: partition), which is somewhat mysterious because it is far inside the body. It separates the thorax (Latin: chest) from the digestive organs below. The diaphragm's fibers begin at its edges, which are attached to the breastbone, the lower ribs and the spine, and they run inward to attach to a central tendon. The "food pipe" (esophagus) and blood vessels pass through openings in the diaphragm to reach the lower body.

When the diaphragm relaxes, it has the shape of two domes, one below each lung (shown by the heavy black line in figure 2.5). When the fibers of the diaphragm tense, they pull the central tendon downward, creating more space in the chest cavity and allowing air to rush in (shown by the dotted line in the figure).

**Figure 2.5**

*The position of the lungs in the rib cage. The dark line shows the relaxed position of the diaphragm, and the dotted line shows the contracted position.*

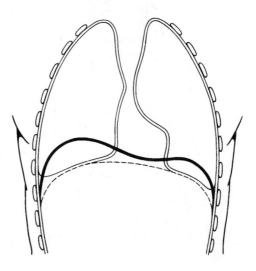

The diaphragm acts without our direct control because it has no proprioceptive nerves of the kind that report sensations of pain or position to the brain. (If the diaphragm were ruptured, for instance, it would not be good for us to feel it because the pain might cause us to stop breathing!)

When the diaphragm acts, it pushes down on the viscera (abdominal organs) and causes the abdominal wall to move outward. When people speak of "breathing from the diaphragm" and pat their tummies, they are really indicating the upper part of the abdominal wall, the epigastrium.

> "To master our breath is to be in control of our bodies and minds."
>
> Thich Nhat Hanh, *The Miracle of Mindfulness* (Boston: Beacon Press, 1987), p. 20

**Breath support**

Now we are ready to consider **breath support,** which has a slightly different meaning from breath control.

During inhalation the external intercostal muscles and the diaphragm work to create more space for the lungs. If they continue working and remain tense, the breath stops moving; no singing takes place.

During exhalation the muscles at the front and sides of the abdomen and/or the ribs move in. If the abdominal and the internal intercostal muscles work together vigorously, they can empty the lungs very quickly, much too quickly for singing.

What happens in fine singing is that the airflow is controlled by using both sets of muscles to oppose each other, as "antagonists." While the exhalation muscles are working, we simultaneously oppose them by keeping the ribs expanded for as long as possible, while the diaphragm continues the downward push that brought the air in. As a result, the air in the lungs and throat is delicately pressurized, just to the degree needed for the musical tone.

The balanced use of these muscles is called "costal-epigastrium breathing" or "sides-and-upper-abdomen breathing." Because we cannot control the diaphragm consciously, we must control it through our conscious decision to breathe out slowly.

An easy way to illustrate the antagonism of the breathing muscles is to put one hand on top of the other with the palms together and push them against each other. One hand pushes down like the diaphragm, while the other pushes up like the upward and inward pull of the abdominal wall. The result is a slow movement that can be precisely controlled.

Our objective is to have this slow, steady movement combined with a well-produced tone. If the vocal tone is breathy, air is being wasted. If the tone sounds pressed, the air is being held in under excessive pressure. When the breath mechanism works perfectly and the tone is also free and balanced, then we can say that we have "breath support" or that the tone is well "supported."

**Phases of breath action**

Here is how we breathe to sing, spelled out in detail. The process has four phases: inhalation, turnaround, exhalation and rest.

1. **Inhalation:** Air enters through the nose, if time allows, or through both the mouth and nose. Sense the throat as open and relaxed. With the ribs already lifted and widened, feel the body opening deeply as the diaphragm descends and the abdominal wall relaxes. Inhale positively and deeply, but comfortably. Imagine the upcoming note so that the voice is ready for the

desired pitch and the right vowel or consonant. Let in enough air to sing the coming phrase, plus a little reserve.

2. **Turnaround:** As your diaphragm reaches its lowest point, there is a split second before the abdominal muscles begin to resist it. The throat remains open, ready to sing.

3. **Exhalation:** Your abdominal wall compresses gently against the resistance of the diaphragm and compresses your air supply. Air rises through the voice box, creating the tone. If the phrase is short, abdominal action alone is enough. For a longer phrase the ribs also move inward slowly without collapsing.

4. **Recovery:** The mechanism returns to its starting position, with the rib cage remaining high, or at least partially lifted. If the music allows time, this can be a rest period, with you breathing normally. If the music goes on quickly, the airflow reverses as quickly as in the turnaround phase.

Often singers feel all four phases as parts of one smooth, continuous cycle. Visualize it as a circular movement or as the lapping of waves on an ocean shore.

## Theories of breath support

All singers use the process described above or some variation of it. Individual singers and teachers explain the process in different ways and emphasize different parts of it in their thinking and singing. This is why equally good singers hold apparently conflicting theories about breath support.

Some singers stress sensations of downward and outward pushing, while others think in terms of more relaxed, flowing movements. Some singers concentrate on the epigastrium area, while others use the whole abdominal wall as a single unit. Others say that the "secret" of support is in the back muscles, which certainly contribute to lifting the ribs. Still others believe that the whole process occurs automatically if our mental concepts of tone are correct. Given such a complex process, it is no wonder that artists use it in a variety of ways.

In action, breath support means keeping the tone flowing evenly, freely, and firmly. At times we may need to concentrate on holding the breath back, while at other times we need to focus on the outward flow.

Furthermore, breath management can be successful only if the tone is efficiently resonant. Breath management and good tone develop together; both must be mastered over an extended period.

## Upside-down breathing

Toddlers breathe correctly, but by adulthood some of us have lost the knack. If "deep breath" means that you lift your chest and pull in your abdomen, as many people do, then you are really taking a high, tense breath. You are "filling up" instead of "breathing deep."

Such "upside-down" breathing causes at least three problems:

1. Your pulled-in abdominal muscles are stiff before you start to sing, so they cannot work to move the air out.

2. When you breathe out, your rib cage falls, affecting your posture and causing tension in the neck muscles.

3. Because the weight of your ribs is providing some of the air compression, you have less flexibility than if the lower muscles were doing the work.

You need to retrain your breathing reflexes, a process that can take several days or several weeks. Start out by relaxing the abdominal muscles during inhalation.

When you sing songs, your mind will be on the words and notes, not on your breathing. The goal of practicing is to make correct breathing action so habitual for you that it continues automatically even when you are not thinking about it. This does not happen overnight. It may take a lot of practice before correct breath action will continue through a whole phrase or song. In the meantime, remind yourself of it often, especially for the beginnings of phrases.

## Bodybuilding

Breathing exercises will benefit anyone who is below normal in physical vitality or weak in chest development. However, bodybuilding in the athletic sense is not our goal. If you are moderately active, you are strong enough for voice study.

Students sometimes wonder out loud whether breathing exercises will thicken their waistlines. Quite the opposite! Good abdominal muscles are essential to a good figure. Incidentally, they also support the back muscles and help us avoid back pains.

Exercise to invigorate and strengthen your body. Running, swimming, yoga, and tai chi are among many exercise programs that help singers. If you work with weights, remember to breathe out when lifting to avoid tensing your throat.

## Coming to terms

Your teacher may want you to know two special words: To sing vocal exercises is to **vocalize** (rhymes with "rise"). A singing exercise has a special name, **vocalise** (rhymes with "lease").

## Exercises

Repeat the stretching exercise from chapter 1. Keep stretches as part of your daily warmup. Try out the sensation of letting your head float toward the ceiling, with your spine dangling from your head and the shoulders and arms relaxed. Feel how pleasant this is, and remind yourself of it often. Add the next exercises.

2.1 **Shoulder Roll.** Both shoulders move in a circular motion back, up, forward and down. Make several circles, then several in the opposite direction. End with the shoulders back and low. Notice that the shoulders are independent from the chest position, whether it is expanded or collapsed. Purpose: to release any tensions that are stiffening the shoulder muscles.

2.2 **Abdominal Action.** Standing erect, raise both arms toward the ceiling so that the rib cage rises. Briefly draw in the abdominal wall and say the consonant sound "sh." Then relax the abdomen outward while air comes into the lungs. In rhythm, alternate one second of "sh" with one second of inhalation. Take turns with a partner, as in figure 2.4, to check whether the muscles are moving in the right direction. Purpose: to sense the bellows-like movement of the abdomen and to overcome any stiffness in this area.

2.3 **Opening the Ribs.** Repeat the second experiment above, using your fists or a partner's (as in figure 2.4) to check first how narrow and then how wide you can make your rib cage (chest). Your ribs should push your fists outward at least one inch on each side. Hold the expanded position for about four seconds and then relax. Purpose: awareness of the potential expansion of the rib cage.

2.4 **Full Breath Action.** Combine deep breathing with smooth arm movements, as in figure 2.6. (The arms stop only at the top and bottom, not in the intermediate positions.)

Phase 1: While you take a slow, deep inhalation through the nose and mouth with your jaw relaxed, raise your arms steadily from your sides, palms down, on a slow count of 1–2–3–4, until they meet over your head.

Phase 2: Keep your arms up for a slow count of 1–2–3–4. The ribs are expanded, the diaphragm is low and the abdominal muscles are relaxed.

Phase 3: Lower your arms slowly while you exhale on a hissing "sh" or "ss" to a slow count of 1–2–3–4. Keep the ribs expanded until the abdominal muscles have finished their lift inward against the diaphragm.

Phase 4: Rest for a count of 1–2–3–4 with an erect posture.

Purpose: to build a habit of sustaining an open rib cage and free, vital breathing with the muscles around the waistline.

When you repeat the exercise in a continuous rhythm, the ribs stay up with the help of the back muscles. Once raised by the first arm lift, the ribs do not need to be lifted again; the arm movement simply reminds us of their position and helps to correct any temporary slump. Practice this daily until your back muscles can sustain a singing posture for several minutes at a time.

**Figure 2.6**

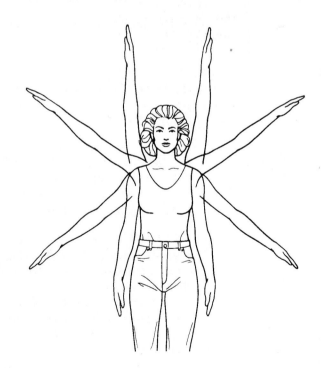

Variations:

**a.** Increase the exhalation count to 6 or 8. Keep the inhalation count at 4 or reduce it to 2.

**b.** Change the "ss" to "zz" or "vv," so that the vocal folds are used for the sound.

**c.** Open your mouth and speak the syllable "huh" on the inhalation. Use a higher pitch than your usual speaking voice.

**d.** Eventually omit the arm action when you no longer need constant reminders of expansion.

**2.5 Bubble Slide.** Through gently closed lips, blow enough air to make your lips vibrate, as if you were blowing bubbles under water. Add vocal tone to make a "bubble slide" like the "hum slide" you learned in chapter 1. (Let the jaw stay loose and in a relaxed, low position.) Purpose: to produce tone with a vigorous and steady breath flow through a comfortable pitch range while eliminating tension from the lips.

Variations:

**a.** Bubble Slide 5th. Practice this on the same musical interval as "hum slide 5th." (Do you remember "Oh, say"?)

**b.** Tongue Roll Slide. Do the action of "rolling an rr" with no vocal tone at first, then add tone to make a slide. Purpose: to produce tone with a vigorous and steady breath flow, while eliminating tension in the tongue.

(If you have trouble producing a "tongue roll," you are not alone. About 10 percent of English-speaking people cannot roll "rr." If you have trouble with the bubble or tongue roll sounds, sing on "oo" in class and keep experimenting with both sounds outside of class.)

**2.6 Starter.** Hum the following rhythm on any comfortable pitch. Be sure that each tone begins and ends precisely in tune. Purpose: to combine agile breath action and accurate attacks on a single pitch, preparing for the quick breaths often needed in songs. (In all exercises, the lower notes are for the lower voices in a voice class.)

Variations: Sing the syllables "see" and "muh" as in "must."

CD 1 Track 3

**2.7 Stepper.** Hum the following pattern, starting on any comfortable pitch. Purpose: to combine agile breath muscle action and accurate attacks on changing pitches.

Variations: Sing the syllables "see" and "muh."

CD 1 Track 4

**2.8 Slow Stepper.** Hum the following pattern, starting on any comfortable pitch. Purpose: same as "Stepper."

Variations: Sing the syllables "see" and "muh."

CD 1 Track 5

Mm   Mm   Mm   Mm   Mm  Mm  Mm  Mm   Mm

*Additional reading*

*For safe ways to improve your physical fitness:*
*Stretching* by Bob Anderson. Shelter Publications (Random House), 1980.

*For excellent photographs of a dissected diaphragm and other vocal organs:*
*Dynamics of the Singing Voice* by Meribeth Bunch. Springer Verlag, 1982.

ALWAYS Maintain correct body and head alignment.

ALWAYS Release abdominal muscles upon inhalation to breathe deeply.

ALWAYS Release the muscles of the tongue, jaw, throat and shoulders on inhalation.

ALWAYS Maintain an open, expanded chest as long as possible while singing.

# Free Tone

*Guiding Questions:*     ***How can I think and talk about vocal tone?***
***How should I start a tone? Stop a tone?***
***How can I learn to produce a pleasing tone at will?***

EACH of us has an individual voice quality—our voices are as unique as our faces. But we can also make many choices about how to use our voices. When we produce tonal qualities we like, we can choose to use them more often and stop using qualities that are less attractive. In this chapter we consider various kinds of tone quality, as well as how to start and stop tones.

## Tone quality

Think of a voice you like to hear. What words describe the way that voice sounds?

Too often, people answer this question with judgmental words like "pretty" or "beautiful" and stop there. We need a wider vocabulary to describe tones we like and don't like. Having more descriptive words will help us make decisions about the sounds we want to produce.

The musical term for tone quality is **timbre** (pronounced like *tam-ber*).

## Descriptive words

Here are some words, arranged in contrasting pairs, that voice teachers sometimes use to describe voices. These words are not scientific terms and not everyone would agree on what they mean, but all of them relate to vocal **technique**.

- agile—stiff
- breathy—clear
- even—uneven
- brassy—velvety
- lyric—dramatic
- crooning—projected

- forced—free
- dull—resonant
- twangy—throaty
- somber—bright
- harsh—mellow
- strong—weak

Here are some even more subjective words that describe the emotional effect of a voice: timid, bold, irritating, boring, soothing, warm, authoritative, ingratiating, shrill.

Do you have other words that describe the effect of certain individuals' voices on you? How would you like other people to describe the effect of your voice?

Consider what these words mean to you. Do they describe some recorded voices you know? Do some of these words describe your singing right now?

**Vocal acoustics**

The science of **acoustics** explains differences in tone quality in terms of the **overtones** that accompany musical tones. Briefly, every vocal tone consists of a basic pitch, the **fundamental,** and also numerous vibrations at higher pitches (overtones) going on simultaneously. Normally, you are not aware of hearing overtones, but you perceive them in terms of tone colors.

If you sing one pitch while changing the vowel from "ah" to "ee," the fundamental does not change, but the overtones do; you are strengthening some overtones and weakening others. The change takes place automatically, by means of slight muscular movements, in response to your mental image of the sound you want to make.

This simple, automatic change demonstrates a basic principle: *You will change and develop your vocal quality by imagining the sounds you want.* Working with our natural voices, most of us have far more possible sounds available than we imagine.

**Tonal goals**

What are some characteristics of a "good" voice, one that we like to hear?

As you read the following list, keep in mind that all of these features of a good voice exist on a scale or continuum. You already have *some* of each of them and you probably want to increase them all.

1. **Audibility.** You would like people to be able to hear you easily in a fairly large room without a microphone. You can meet this goal just by learning to apply energy to your voice and to remove physical tensions. Vocal strength is a by-product of good vocal habits, not a goal in itself.

2. **Resonance.** A quality of "ring" in the voice results from strong overtones, particularly certain ones at a very high pitch that affect the human ear pleasantly. Even low male voices require these high overtones at around 2,800–3,200 Herz (vibrations per second). A voice without them seems dull, lacking in beauty and carrying power. Again, any healthy voice can develop enough "ring" for good singing.

3. **Clarity.** We prefer a clear tone with no extra noises (for instance, breathiness) that interfere with the overtones.

4. **Intelligibility.** This is clarity of consonant and vowel formation. Anyone who really cares about communicating with an audience can achieve this with intelligent hard work.

5. **Pure intonation.** Good musicianship requires an ability to start, continue, and stop a tone on pitch, without sliding up or down unintentionally. (If you suspect you might be tone-deaf, look up this topic in chapter 12.)

6. **Dynamic variety.** Musical expression requires an ability to sing softer and louder, with smooth changes from one level to another.

7. **Color variety.** Dramatic expression requires an ability to change vocal tone color (timbre), with "bright" tones (stronger high partials) and "dark" tones (weaker high partials) and other qualities produced in response to your imagination and feelings.

8. **Vibrato.** A well-produced voice is capable of regular, gentle pulsations that enliven the tone. More is said about vibrato later in this chapter.

9. **Range.** Most songs require more than an octave (8 scale tones). "The Star-Spangled Banner" requires a twelfth (12 scale tones). A professional singer is expected to sing two octaves (15 scale tones) or more with comfort and good quality, in addition to weaker tones below and above that range. In fact, every healthy voice has a range of more than two octaves, needing only the skill and practice to make those tones usable. Range, like loudness, is a by-product of good vocal habits, not a goal in itself.

**10. Ease/freedom.** Good singing takes both mental and physical effort, but the audience wants the singer to look, as well as sound, comfortable.

For each of these characteristics of a good voice, imagine a scale from 1 to 10. If you rate your voice on a characteristic, does the rating stay the same every day? How big is the variation between the best and poorest days? We would like to improve the best days and the consistency at the same time.

Which areas are already easy for you? Do some areas seem difficult to develop? Don't worry. All of them will improve with practice.

## Attacks and releases

The start of a musical tone is called the **attack.** Good tone starts with a good attack. A good attack starts with imagining a tone clearly—pitch, quality, and dynamic level—before you sing it.

If an attack is shaky or out of tune, the whole phrase may be out of tune. Likewise, if an attack is harsh and tense, the tone is apt to remain tense to the end of the phrase. Aim for a free, clear, effortless tone on the attack.

**Release** is the ending of a musical tone. A good release results from a mental decision to stop or reverse the flow of breath. Often one phrase follows closely after another. The release of one phrase is the in-breath that prepares for the next phrase.

## What the vocal folds do

Moving air causes a tone by vibrating the vocal folds, commonly known as the vocal cords. (Scientists now prefer the term folds because it better describes their shape.) Chapter 11 describes them in some detail, but at this point you need to know four things:

## Can I be a professional singer?

If there are great possibilities for developing your voice, does that mean that anyone can become a great singer? No, of course not. Everyone can learn to swing a baseball bat, but not everyone can play in the major leagues. A professional singer possesses all of the basic resources listed above and uses them with superior skill, refinement, and imagination.

We can hardly begin to list what goes into a major singing career: years of study, strong musical skills, superior health, vivid personality, artistic creativity, dramatic flair, and much more. Business sense, unflagging ambition, ability to choose the right teachers, coaches, and agents, and, yes, money, are also ingredients in most singing careers. Furthermore, not everyone who could have a singing career wants one enough to live the demanding life of a performer.

But if you are not going to be a professional singer, is your voice worth developing? Yes, definitely. Set your own goals and decide what priority singing has in your life. Your goal may be to entertain your friends, sing in a barbershop chorus, sing at worship services, or participate in a community chorus or theater. These are all realizable goals. Between singing at home and professional stardom there are an infinite number of possibilities for satisfying artistic self-expression. With time, work, training, and imagination you may go much further than you imagine right now.

1. The vocal folds can be brought together over the windpipe, closing it so tightly that no air can enter or leave the lungs.
2. They are drawn apart when we breathe in and out normally, allowing air to pass between them (as in figure 11.2 on page 78).
3. The vocal folds come together during singing, but loosely enough so that air can still escape between them and make them vibrate. Tiny puffs of air passing between them cause the sound waves that resonate in the throat and mouth to make tone.
4. The vocal folds are living tissue, mostly muscle, and have a delicate covering similar to the inside of your mouth. If they are infected or abused (for instance, by coughing), the healing process makes them swell temporarily so that the edges do not meet smoothly. In this case you will hear a hoarse or raspy tone or no tone at all. When this happens, stop singing and rest your voice. Read chapter 11 for more advice.

**Three methods of attack**

What you now know about the vocal folds makes it easy to understand that there are three methods of attack: glottal, breathy, and clean.

1. **Glottal attack** occurs when the vocal folds are held closed and air pressure pushes them apart to start the tone. If the resulting sound is explosive and coughlike, it can be tiring to the vocal folds.
2. **Breathy attack** occurs when air passes between the vocal folds before they meet and begin vibrating. It sounds like an unwanted "ha."
3. **Clean attack** occurs when the movement of air and the closure of the vocal folds are practically simultaneous.

Fortunately if we have a clear mental concept of the desired tone, the body coordinates this delicate adjustment automatically for us.

If you cannot achieve a clean attack, ask your teacher for advice. Your vocal folds may be swollen (see #4 above) so that they need rest or medical treatment.

Some people use the vocal folds to close off the windpipe and pressurize the air in the lungs, as when lifting a heavy weight or chopping wood. This is another cause of wear and tear on the vocal folds. Learn to exercise without holding your breath. (Weight lifters have a good slogan: "Blow the weight up.")

Also, some people habitually speak with hard glottal stops, so that every word beginning with a vowel starts with a little coughing sound. This abuses the vocal folds, as all speech therapists agree.

Here's how to test for harmful glottal attacks: Stop both ears with your fingers, then hum a tone in an easy range. If there is a glottal attack, you will hear and feel the click or coughlike attack. To change this habit, temporarily start each tone with a "silent h," a little breath that escapes ahead of the tone. Drop the silent h when you no longer need it.

**Three methods of release**

Just as there are three methods of attack, there are three ways to end a tone:

1. **Stopped release.** The vocal folds close together tightly to stop both the tone and the breath; the needless friction of the vocal folds may be harmful.

2. **Breathy release.** The vocal folds separate and stop the tone, but air is still flowing out; there may be unwanted noise.
3. **Clean release.** The diaphragm drops, the vocal folds separate, and air flows into the lungs simultaneously.

Obviously the most efficient release is the "clean" one, in which the ending of one tone simultaneously begins the preparation for the next. When you sing exercises, become aware of which method you are using.

## Resonance

If we could hear a tone that comes directly from the vocal folds, it would sound buzzy and unpleasant. In reality, before we hear sound waves from the vocal folds, they are transformed by resonation.

**Resonation** means the *intensification of a tone by sympathetic vibration*. **Sympathetic vibration** is the *tendency of air in an enclosed or partially enclosed space to vibrate in response to a musical tone*. In singing, the voice gains strength and quality from bouncing back and forth in our **resonators:** the throat, mouth and other spaces of the neck and head. They are the "partially enclosed spaces" in which desirable sound waves are reinforced and others die away.

Resonance makes your voice louder by concentrating vibratory energy onto specific frequencies (pitches). In that process, resonance strengthens the overtones that give your voice its basic quality. They also produce vowel colors that change as the shape and size of your throat and mouth openings change.

A resonant tone can be felt as vibrations in the important resonators. When you hear a tone you like, pay attention not only to the sound but also to how the vibrations feel in your mouth, throat, and head. Remembering these sensations will help you re-create the same tone in the future.

All musical instruments use the principle of resonance. Here are examples:
A plucked guitar string makes a tone that resonates in the body of the guitar.
A trumpeter's vibrating lips make a tone that resonates inside the horn.
Can you give other examples?

## Increasing your resonance

Having stronger resonance means that your voice has more carrying power, more ability to seize a listener's attention, more power to communicate your feelings.

Do you remember hearing a baby's cry? It instantly grabs your attention. Other powerful communicators are laughs, groans, whimpers, and sighs. These are all wordless emotional messages, and our brains instinctively give them attention. Singing takes some of the emotional power of these natural sounds, gives them musical form, and combines them with words. This understanding of the nature of singing gives us clues to discovering our best resonance.

Resonance arises instinctively when we:

- Really want to communicate;
- Use emotional energy and enthusiasm;
- Put physical energy into our sound;
- Get rid of physical and emotional blocks.

Experiment with the sentences that follow, speaking them out loud. Use enough energy to be heard in a large room. See how many different emotional meanings you can give to each one.

- Will you sing a solo?
- You should have been there!
- So you are the one!
- Hey, you, get away from my car!

Can you make up other sentences that call up emotional responses? At this stage, let your feelings be the key to vocal resonance. In later chapters you will learn more about technical aspects of resonance.

## Feeling and hearing

While your mental concepts about singing are developing, you can rely on the two senses that control singing, *feeling* and *hearing*, to know when you are on the right track. Ask yourself these questions as you sing:

- Does your throat feel comfortable and relaxed? If you feel tension, pressure, or pain in your throat, there is clearly something wrong.
- Is the tone ringing, intense, and efficient in resonance?
- Is the vowel clear and pure?
- Is the tone on pitch?
- Do you feel that the tone can be manipulated up or down in range, louder or softer in dynamics, darker or brighter in tone color? A lack of flexibility in these respects is a signal of unwanted tension.

Your best resonance usually goes along with a sense of freedom and relaxation. Tensions in the tongue, jaw muscles, and neck interfere with ease, quality, and control of singing. Other body tensions may also interfere sooner or later. In a healthy throat, if the extrinsic (outer) muscles are relaxed, the intrinsic (inner) muscles of the larynx can do their job properly.

## How to vocalize

Repeat the exercises from chapters 1 and 2. Each chapter adds to your repertoire of exercises that help you get ready to sing every day, even when you don't feel motivated. Especially repeat "Abdominal Action," "Opening the Ribs," and "Full Breath Action" until you feel confident that you breathe correctly for singing at any time, at will. Sing the voice exercises with an awareness of attack and release.

Notice that the new exercises given below, nos. 3.2–3.6, emphasize the hum consonants, *n* and *m*. They prepare a resonant intensity for the tone and a feeling of the tone resonating high in the head.

The new exercises also emphasize a neutral vowel sound, *Uh*, that is formed with a uniformly open vocal passage. *Uh* is the sound that our vocal instrument makes when it is most relaxed and not shaped to produce some other more distinctive vowel. Think of *Uh* as a free and ringing tone (Up!), never muffled (Dull!).

When the tone changes from *Uh* to another vowel, let the change be as smooth as possible, using a minimum of change in your resonating spaces.

Use a vital and comfortable tone with a medium dynamic level, either medium loud (mf) or medium soft (mp).

## What pitches to sing

Explore your voice, trying many different pitches—medium, low and high. Exercises can begin on any pitch that is comfortable in your range. Keep in mind that your purpose is to warm up the singing instrument and not to challenge it right away.

Start each exercise somewhat above your normal speaking pitch. Sing it twice or more. Notice how it improves with repetition. Transpose it downward several times to lower keys. Repeat the exercise on a somewhat higher starting pitch and again move downward several times. Repeat a key whenever you feel you can improve the tone. Start over again in a higher key, if you can do so without a sense of reaching or straining.

This is a strategy for exploring your full range with ease. "Take what the voice gives you," as voice teacher Oren Brown expresses it, rather than force the voice to sing a wider range.

## Vocalizing for vocal fitness

Plan ahead so that singing is part of your normal day. If you sing actively on six days of the week, the voice will benefit from resting on the seventh day.

At this early stage, practice in short stretches of 10–15 minutes. Practice with full concentration, not absentmindedly. You are building new mental and muscular habits, and this must be done thoughtfully for the best results.

Between lessons, you are your own teacher. You must understand the goal of each exercise and regulate your own practicing to achieve your goals. You must decide how many times to repeat an exercise and how high or low, how loudly or softly to sing. Singing with energy, purpose, and intelligent thought will produce guaranteed progress. Singing thoughtlessly allows mistakes to become habits that cause real problems later.

Thirty to sixty minutes of singing every day is plenty for your vocal development at this stage. If you have more time, spend it on learning about music, listening to recordings of fine singers, studying poetry and drama, acting and languages. If you are in a choir or other singing group, take this into account as you plan your singing day. Your total singing time should not exceed two hours on any given day, including group rehearsals and your personal practice time.

## Exercises

3.1 **Panting.** Place the fingertips on the stomach wall in the epigastrium area just below the breastbone. With the chest comfortably high, quickly inhale a vigorous breath (the fingertips move outward). Release the breath suddenly, speaking a "sh" sound (the fingertips move inward). Repeat vigorously and rhythmically in a series of panting pulsations. Purpose: to induce a sensation of lively breath muscle action and quick inhalation.

The next exercises use a clean attack as we usually use it in normal **legato** singing. Purpose: to produce a free, efficient, uniform tone with a clean attack and release in various musical situations.

3.2 **Hum-Tones.**                    3.3 **Down Five.**

CD 1 Tracks 6 & 7

Nn - uh - ee _____          Nn - uh - ee _____
Nn - uh - oh _____          Nn - uh - oh _____

**3.4 Singles.** Begin each tone exactly on pitch. End the tone with the mouth and the breath passage both open, not closing either the mouth or the throat.

CD 1 Track 8

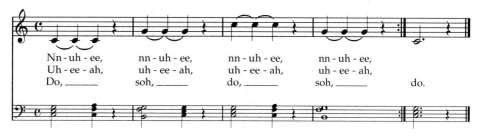

Nn - uh - ee,    nn - uh - ee,    nn - uh - ee,    nn - uh - ee,
Uh - ee - ah,    uh - ee - ah,    uh - ee - ah,    uh - ee - ah,
Do, _____    soh, _____    do, _____    soh, _____    do.

**3.5 Dee-Dees.** Start each syllable with a light, quick tongue movement. Check that every D consonant is exactly on pitch (you can hear this best by stopping one ear with a finger while you sing). The jaw does not need to move. Take a breath at each rest. Purpose: to loosen the tongue and bring it forward while establishing that voiced consonants are sung on pitch.

CD 1 Track 9

Dee-dee-dee-dee, dee-dee-dee-dee,   dee-dee-dee-dee, dee-dee-dee-dee,   dee-dee-dee-dee, dee.

**3.6 Tune-up.** Sing the quick syllables lightly, pronouncing *m*'s and *n*'s quickly. Keep the jaw out of action as much as possible. In voice classes, sing in two parts. Purpose: to prepare for sustaining long tones with continued vitality and freshness.

CD 1 Track 10

Mee-meh-mah-moh-moo,    Mee-meh-mah-moh-moo,    Mee-meh-mah-moh-moo.
Nee-neh - nah - noh - noo,    Nee-neh - nah - noh - noo,    Nee-neh - nah - noh - noo.

**3.7 Yummies.** The glide sound "Y" brightens the tone. Purpose: to develop a relaxed, resonant tone with a sense of high, forward resonance. Suggestion: In voice class sing this in canon, with half of the voices beginning on beat 3.

CD 1 Track 11

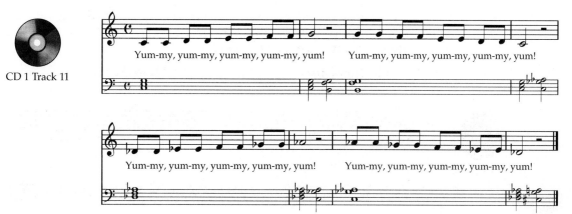

Yum-my, yum-my, yum-my, yum-my, yum!    Yum-my, yum-my, yum-my, yum-my, yum!

Yum-my, yum-my, yum-my, yum-my, yum!    Yum-my, yum-my, yum-my, yum-my, yum!

*Additional*
*listening*

*Learn about different kinds of tone quality by listening to recordings of singing styles that are unfamiliar to you. Some examples might be: Italian opera, Native American songs, Beijing opera, Renaissance music using a countertenor voice, Wagnerian opera, music from India, 1930s jazz and blues, and various pop styles. Examples should be available in any public library listening area.*

ALWAYS Use a clear attack and clear release to begin and end phrases.

ALWAYS Think a high resonance that adjusts freely for vowel and pitch changes.
> (Resonance cannot be put in one spot—each vowel and pitch feels different even though always high.)

ALWAYS Release the tongue and jaw as freely as when you are singing *Uh.*

ALWAYS Maintain a core of resonance (ring) in the tone.

# Changing Resonances in Your Voice

**Guiding Questions:** *Why do the upper notes of my voice sound and feel different from the lower notes?*
*What kinds of voices are there, and what kind do I have?*
*How can I make my voice more resonant?*

Have you noticed that some parts of your voice feel different from others? Can you sing some notes in more than one way?

Untrained singers often feel uncomfortable because some notes of their voices are weaker than other notes. Let's learn about them and find out how to work with them.

## Chest or head?

Try this experiment: Place your hands on your ribs and sing a strong tone on a fairly low pitch. What do you feel? You probably feel vibrations in your bones. Now keep your hands on your ribs and sing a high, light note. Do you still feel the vibrations? Probably not. Now start on a high note and let the pitch slide downward. As the pitch goes down, you will reach a pitch where you feel the ribs begin to vibrate again.

Centuries ago singers noticed these sensations. Not knowing about the vocal folds, they thought that certain tones originated in the chest and others in the head. This is not true—chest vibration is simply a response to tone, a sympathetic vibration. However, many singers still speak of "chest voice" and "head voice" because of the sensations that accompany our low and high registers.

## Blending registers

Luckily our voices have many qualities available, not just two. When we imagine tones, the vocal folds adjust themselves subtly, changing in length, thickness, shape, and the amount of surface contact along their edges. Chest voice and head voice don't just change like the flick of a switch. Good singers continually mix and blend their tones when they decide how loud or soft to sing and what quality to use. They do this simply by imagining the tone quality they want to use.

Our ideal goal in classical singing is to have all notes equal in quality and strength. This could be described as a voice with one **register,** meaning that the highest and lowest notes and all the notes in between sound alike. Some voice teachers speak of a one-register voice that is either a rare gift of nature or the result of years of training. Others think that a one-register voice is an illusion that a skillful singer creates.

Whatever one may think about registers, most students are well aware of unequal tones in their voices. A majority of singers are aware of three registers:

27

1. Head or light mechanism;
2. Medium or blended mechanism; and
3. Chest or heavy mechanism.

Three registers were recognized in the 1840s by Manuel Garcia II, the first person who ever used a dental mirror to observe the vocal folds during singing. In *Hints on Singing* he offered this classic definition: "A register is a series of consecutive homogeneous sounds produced by one mechanism. . . ."

Other theories of registers also have followers. Dr. R. Berton Coffin agreed that vocal folds act differently in various registers, but he showed that there are also acoustical distinctions between them. On an acoustical basis he identified 11 registers, of which the lowest ones are used only by basses and the highest only by sopranos.

All of these differing theories still agree:

1. Men do most of their singing in the chest voice, blending to the medium and head for their higher notes.
2. Women do most of their singing in the head voice, blending to medium and chest for their lower notes.
3. The registers overlap a great deal, allowing us to make choices according to the tone quality and loudness desired.

## Your speaking pitch level

Which register do you like to use when you sing? Which is your strongest?

Let's start by thinking about your speaking voice. Is it high or low? Our modern culture favors low speaking voices. Parents tell children to keep their voices down. Girls may or may not realize that their voices drop by three or four tones during puberty, but they definitely feel more grown-up when their voices lose the shrillness of childhood. When adolescent boys' voices drop an octave or more, their friends and family praise them for sounding like men. Both women and men are apt to respond to positive feedback by speaking low, sometimes even lower than is natural.

You can test the pitch of your own speaking voice (perhaps with your teacher's help). Speak a syllable that ends with the consonant *m, n* or *ng*. Prolong the consonant and listen to the pitch it makes. Match the pitch on a piano. You may be surprised at how low it is. Many women speak below middle C, even though they sing much higher.

What is the best pitch for speaking? Speech teachers recommend that you use a habitual pitch about one-third of the way up the scale from your lowest possible speaking tone to your highest. Over the next few days notice how high your voice goes when you are excited or surprised. The pitch of your voice when you laugh or cough also provides a clue to the most natural pitch for your speaking voice. When you find the best pitch level, it will help you speak without fatigue. Because your speaking pitch will vary with expression, it is not necessary to measure it exactly.

Does speaking too low or too high cause any problems? Yes, it can cause vocal fatigue and even voice loss. Also, our wish to speak low means that many persons start out singing in the heavy voice and feel uncomfortable about experimenting with the blended and light voices. The opposite is less often true, but some students need encouragement to use the strength that the heavy voice will give to their low notes.

Experiment to strengthen resonance in the weaker parts of your voice. A goal of voice training is to balance and strengthen all of the notes in your range.

## What kind of voice?

If you ask your teacher, "What kind of voice do I have?" you may receive an answer right away, or your teacher may wait to see how your voice develops over a period of time. A choral director must classify voices quickly during auditions, but voice teachers prefer to take more time.

Poor vocal habits and wrong ideas about singing can hide the natural quality of your voice so that it takes weeks or months to emerge. Some students imitate a favorite singer whose quality is not at all like their own. Because they like another person's style, they unintentionally falsify their own sound.

Imitation is a valid way of learning to sing, but only if the sound you imitate is right for you. Your voice is going to change and grow, but if you try to change it into something that is against its physical nature, there can be problems ahead. There are serious risks, for instance, if a woman, to help out her choir, sings tenor all the time. If you use one part of your range exclusively, you run a risk of overusing it and making the rest of your voice seem feeble by comparison. A good way to use your voice is to balance the use of the registers.

## Voice types

To answer the question "What kind of voice do I have?" you need to know what names are given to different voices. In fact, voices have somewhat different names in different kinds of music.

Choral music uses four kinds of voices: **soprano, alto, tenor,** and **bass.** Any section can also divide into higher and lower voices, for instance, first altos and second altos (abbreviated Alto I and Alto II).

Opera requires more precise classifications of voices. Sopranos who specialize in singing notes above the staff are called coloratura or lyric-coloratura sopranos. Lower-voiced women are divided into **mezzo-sopranos,** who sing almost as high as sopranos, and **contraltos,** who specialize in low singing. Lower-voiced men are similarly divided into **baritones, bass baritones,** and **basses.** In addition, operatic voices can be further classified by words that describe what the voice does best or how it sounds, such as **lyric** or **dramatic.** Opera fans love to discuss what kind of voice is best for a certain role, based on their interpretation of the character.

Broadway musical theater uses a different concept in classifying women's voices. Most roles require a woman to **belt,** which means to sing at a high energy level, especially in a low range. Some belting roles go even lower than an operatic contralto. On Broadway a blended or head tone is called **legitimate** or just **legit.** A casting notice might read: "Must sing both belt and legit." The Broadway concept is that a woman chooses between belt and legit singing according to her natural ability, training, and personal preference. (Male voices can also belt, but the contrast between belt and legit is less striking in male voices because of the prevalence of chest tones.)

**Table 4.1**
Types of voices

| | Choral | Operatic/Concert | Pop/Broadway |
|---|---|---|---|
| *Women* | | | |
| (high) | | Coloratura soprano | |
| | Soprano | Soprano | Legit/soprano |
| | Alto | Mezzo-soprano | Belt |
| (low) | | Contralto | |
| *Men* | | | |
| (high) | Tenor | Tenor | Tenor |
| | | Baritone | |
| | Bass | Bass-baritone | Baritone |
| (low) | | Bass | |

## Belt and pop singing

Is belting dangerous? Many voice teachers think so, especially for young singers whose muscular development is not complete. Some voice teachers reject belting because they simply do not like the sound. Yet, if you accept a role in a musical, you may have to do some belting.

Certainly, belting is a high-energy way of singing and carries some risks just like other high-energy activities and sports. Some singers belt well and sing professionally on Broadway for years without losing their voices. Others belt poorly, ignore trouble signs such as hoarseness and pain, and lose their voices in a short time.

The same goes for both women and men who sing rock, jazz, or other kinds of popular music. Singing aloud with loud electronic instruments causes many young singers to force their voices and even lose them. (Many rock musicians wear fitted earplugs to lessen the damage to their hearing. Many rock singers use in-the-ear feedback devices to hear themselves.)

If you sing popular or Broadway music, please don't keep it a secret. Your teacher can help you to sing without hurting your voice.

## Vibrato

Vibrato is a gentle, regular pulsation that is heard in both the intensity and the pitch of a tone. A good vibrato makes the voice sound free and relaxed, warm and expressive. We listen for vibrato as a natural part of a freely produced voice.

Vocal science has not yet identified a single cause for vibrato, but it makes sense to believe that it is caused mainly by a pulsation or pressure variation in the breath. Because the whole breath system is involved, the pulsation is not felt or seen in any one part of the body.

As with other characteristics of good singing, we must imagine a pleasing vibrato in order to produce one. If you have never used vibrato, it may take a while before you achieve the right balance of energy and relaxation to let it happen spontaneously. If you sing a tone with vibrato, take notice of it and encourage it to reappear.

Classical singing uses vibrato in nearly every tone, but other styles use it differently. Country music singers seldom use it, while some gospel and blues singers like a pitch variation of more than a half-tone. Jazz stylists, particularly, add and subtract vibrato at will for expression.

Sometimes we hear a vibrato that is too fast or slow (a normal speed is six to seven pulses per second), or too wide (more than one-quarter tone above and below the desired pitch), or one that pulses loud and soft like a bleat. Singers use the word **tremolo** to describe any such unpleasant vibratos. They can be corrected by improving breath support and learning the right balance of vitality and relaxation in singing.

Some singers consciously inhibit their vibrato. These are some reasons that I have heard:

*Someone said that if I try to use vibrato it will be unnatural; I should wait until I'm older and it will come naturally.*

False: The vibrato you have in your teens is yours. Use it with pride.

*The choir director said my vibrato made my voice stick out.*

Translation: One mature voice among other immature voices caused a problem that the director didn't have time to solve. It would be better to improve the weaker voices than to stifle the stronger one.

*I don't want my voice to sound "operatic" and affected.*

Don't worry, you won't go overboard. Try singing with vibrato, and you will find that your friends like it.

Some students can begin to use vibrato immediately, once they allow it to happen.

## Exercises

These exercises further help to eliminate physical tensions that can interfere with resonant singing. While not everyone has the same tensions, all of these exercises help to warm up the voice. Combine them with exercises from chapters 1 and 2.

**4.1 Mental Messages.** Imagine the muscles under your eyes completely relaxed, the lips loose, the tongue lying forward in the mouth, and the jaw hanging freely. One by one, send mental messages to the cheeks, lips, tongue, jaw and neck muscles to relax.

**4.2 Jaw Wobble.** Using both hands, move your jaw *gently* from side to side. The hands supply the movement, not the jaw muscles, which remain perfectly loose. If you cannot do this, work patiently with a mirror until you discover how to release the muscles that are holding the jaw stiff. (If this causes any discomfort, stop immediately and consult your dentist.)

**4.3 Jaw Flopper.** Shake your head easily from side to side, with the jaw and lips swinging loosely from side to side.

**4.4 Hand Shake.** Shake your hands loosely from the wrists, dispelling any tension in your arms.

Let your voice warm up on some of the vocal exercises from chapters 1 through 3 before going on to the next exercises. Sing all exercises in several different keys. Some exercises cover a range of a full octave. Do you have a better understanding now of why high tones feel different from low tones?

**4.5 Little Arches.** Even before you sing the first note, have the first *two* notes of each phrase in mind. If you do this, the upward jump will be in tune and the tones will connect smoothly. Purpose: to use breath and resonance evenly in a small melodic pattern. (High voices: Sing this in F major, starting on B♭.)

CD 1 Track 12

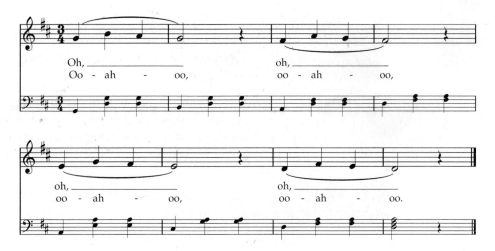

**4.6 Octave Flip.** Start on any high, light note that comes easily to your voice. "Flip" to the low note and back up, with the sudden switch that one hears in yodeling. Transpose downward a few times, then start over on a higher pitch. (Women: use head voice. Men: use falsetto.) Purpose: to sense a contrast between the light and heavy registers when they are not mixed.

CD 1 Track 13

**4.7 Octave Sigh.** Start on any high note that comes easily to your voice. Sing the word "sigh." On beat 3 let your voice slide slowly down one octave, not stopping on any tone along the way. Feel as if you are sighing. Transpose downward by half-steps a few times, then start over on a higher pitch. Purpose: to smooth out and minimize the differences between the light and heavy registers, mixing them gradually on the way down.

CD 1 Track 14

**4.8 5-Note Bee-Dee's.** Start on any easy note around the mid-point of your range. Transpose downward to your lowest comfortable range. Purpose: to sense an easy, bright resonance, combined with quick, light articulation.

CD 1 Track 15

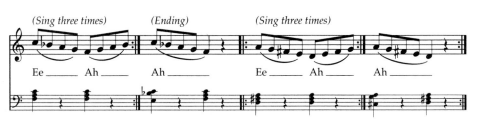

Bee - dee - bee - dee - bee - dee - bee - dee - bee - dee - bee - dee - bee.

**4.9 5-Note Ee-Ah's.** Start on any easy note around the mid-point of your range. Sense the brightness of the first vowel, and let the brightness carry into the second vowel. Transpose downward to your lowest comfortable range, then start over again a little higher. Purpose: to sense the way one vowel can brighten another.

CD 1 Track 16

*(Sing three times)*     *(Ending)*     *(Sing three times)*

Ee _____ Ah _____     Ah _____     Ee _____ Ah _____     Ah _____

**4.10 Focusers.** Try these combinations of syllables, which will help to "center" your vocal energy. Notice which syllables work best for you and practice them daily. Sing in several comfortable keys. Purpose: to feel the relationship between vowel and resonance, as well as the role of initial consonants in preparing tone.

CD 1 Track 17

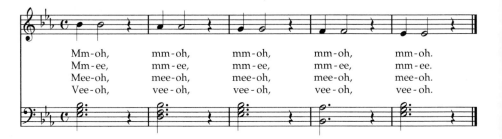

Mm-oh,     mm-oh,     mm-oh,     mm-oh,     mm-oh.
Mm-ee,     mm-ee,     mm-ee,     mm-ee,     mm-ee.
Mee-oh,    mee-oh,    mee-oh,    mee-oh,    mee-oh.
Vee-oh,    vee-oh,    vee-oh,    vee-oh,    vee-oh.

**Additional reading**

*For tips on improving your speaking voice:*

*Is Your Voice Telling on You?* by Daniel R. Boone. Singular Publishing Group, 1991.

*For more about the technique and style of pop singing:*

*Born to Sing* by Elisabeth Howard and Howard Austin. Vocal Power Institute, 2123 N. Topanga Canyon Blvd., Topanga, CA 90290, 1-800-829-SONG; (book and CD package or videocassette).

ALWAYS "Place the voice as high as the highest note in the phrase." (Quoted from Mathilde Marchesi, a great voice teacher of the 1800s.)

ALWAYS Allow the *brain and the breath* to do your work (rather than tense muscles).

ALWAYS Encourage an expressive, even vibrato on both short and long tones.

# Preparing a Song

**Guiding Questions:** *How can I choose a song that I will enjoy singing?*
*What is the best way to learn the words and music of a song so that I can sing it expressively and confidently?*

EVEN though there is much more to learn about vocal technique, you can begin to use what you know in singing songs. This book contains a large variety of songs that are fun to sing. They also give you an opportunity to learn more about your voice and about singing.

## Choosing a song

Your teacher may choose your first song or else help you choose it. Perhaps you have a chance to select among several songs. If you are making the choice, consider the following advice:

- *Choose words that you can believe in.* If words don't make sense to you, they are harder to learn and harder to sing expressively.

- *Begin with easier songs,* so that you can pay attention to improving your tone quality.

- *Choose a short song over a longer one.* At first, you will learn more by doing several short songs than by sticking to one long one. Also, your teacher can give you more help in lessons if you sing a short song several times rather than a long song once.

After you have done several easy songs the time will come to apply your skill to longer, more challenging songs. But now the main goal is to learn, quickly and pleasurably, how to sing.

In order to be sure you like the chosen song, you will want to *hear* it right away. Use a cassette recorder to tape the song in class. You can sing through some or all of the song, but only as long as it is easy and fun to do so. Let any hard parts wait until later.

Make a mental note of *something you really like* in your song because you are going to spend a lot of time with it. Does it appeal to you because of a mood, a mental picture, or an idea? Because of a graceful melody or a lively rhythm? Because of its quaintness or its modern sound?

You have made friends with your new song—why not just start singing it? Because you don't want to make mistakes that will turn into habits. Also, singing in an insecure, uncertain way brings on tension that can turn into bad vocal habits. On the other hand, patient work now will pay off in confidence and success later, at performance time.

## Learning the music

How you learn songs will depend on your musical experience and on your learning style. Here are some ideas about learning a song, using "Love Will Find Out the Way," found on page 124, as an example.

If you can read notes or play an instrument, this song will be easy for you to learn. If not, you can hear the song on the compact disc that comes with this book. You will notice that the piano plays all of the melody notes. We say that the piano "doubles" the voice in this song. Doubling makes the song easy to learn but also limits the amount of freedom you have to interpret the song in your own way. (If you learn a song in which the piano part does not double the melody, use a cassette recorder to record the melody while someone plays it for you.)

First, take a good look at the song's heading. It says that this is a traditional English song with a melody that was published as long ago as 1652. Country folk have sung this tune for a long time, and the mood and style of the song are clear: vigorous, straightforward, uncomplicated. Of course, most folk songs can be sung without any accompaniment; the piano part is added especially for this book.

Now let's look at the musical notation. (Chapter 12 will be helpful if you have never read notes before. You can skip ahead and read it anytime.)

Rhythm provides a lot of this song's energy. The underlying rhythm is in three-beat patterns—musicians call this **triple meter**—meaning that a strong, accented beat is always followed by two equal, weaker beats. In the **score** (written music) each accented beat is shown by a vertical line before it, called a **bar line** or measure line. Even without the **meter signature** of 3/4, it is obvious that many measures contain three syllables of text.

While you listen to the melody, it is a good idea to "keep time" actively. This helps you develop a physical relationship to the music so that your rhythm will be steady and clear when you sing.

Beating time with your hand is a natural response, but it is easy to forget which beat is which. Here is a better way to keep time:

Sit at a table and tap on it with one hand or both. Tap the beats this way:

beat 1 near the book,

beat 2 a few inches away, and

beat 3 further away.

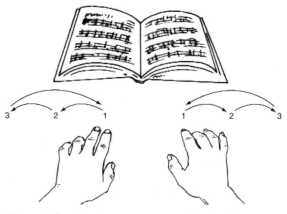

At the end of each measure return your hand to the starting position; the movement of your hand through the air gives extra energy to beat 1. If you use both hands, move them away from your body on beats 1, 2 and 3; after beat 3 both hands move back to the starting position.

Remember to tap the basic, steady beat. At this point, don't try to beat the shorter and longer notes in the melody.

Try tapping the meter steadily while listening to the melody. Most measures have notes on all three beats, but sometimes you are tapping a beat that does not have a note on it. For instance, in measure 3 the second note is lengthened so that "the" comes not on beat 3 but after it. In measure 4, "waves" fills up two beats and you have time to breathe on beat 3.

While you tap the meter steadily through the whole melody, you are learning it by ear. When you feel that the melody is familiar, try singing it on nonsense syllables. "Doo-doo-doo" and "La-la-la" are syllables that work well at this stage. (If you have learned to read notes and use the do-re-mi syllables, this is the time to use that knowledge.)

Singing the melody on syllables is called **vocalizing,** and it is a significant part of learning a song. Repeat this step enough times so that you feel perfectly confident about the melody. Your voice should feel comfortable and your breath support should be working well before you sing the words of the song.

You may have noticed that the melody of this song begins with a four-measure phrase that is repeated immediately and that the whole melody is only four phrases long. The melody will be sung again for every stanza of the words. Most music has such repetition patterns that help us learn the music.

## Learning the words

A wise person once said that *all* songs are love songs, and this song is about the power of love. Let's begin with the poetry. Do you like poetry? If you're not sure, at least keep an open mind. Every song begins as a poem. Without words, what would we sing about?

Step 1. *Read all the way through the words* to get a general idea of the meaning.

Step 2. *Write out the words by hand in poetic form.* Why? When words are spread out in a printed song, you can't see clearly how they fit together to form a poem and tell a story. Here is the first stanza of "Love Will Find Out the Way."

> Over the mountains
> And over the waves,
> Under the fountains
> And under the graves,
> Under floods that are deepest,
> Which Neptune obey,
> Over rocks that are steepest,
> Love will find out the way.

Finish writing out the other stanzas of the poem. As you can see, every line rhymes with one other line. Knowing this makes it easier to memorize the poem.

Step 3. *Make sure you understand every word.* One way to make sure is to **paraphrase** the poem, which means to express every idea of the poem in your own words. Work out your paraphrase either on paper or in your mind, so that the meaning of every word and phrase you sing will be clear to you. Paraphrases are in prose because only the meanings matter, not the rhymes and rhythms. Change as many words as you can without changing the meaning. A paraphrase is usually longer than the poem because a good poem is concentrated into as few words as possible.

Your paraphrase will be different from anyone else's because a poetic phrase can have more than one meaning. A good poem always communicates on more than one level, including the musical effects of rhythm and rhyme.

Are there unfamiliar words? Use a dictionary. (Do you need to look up Neptune?) No one knows every word in the English language, and even a current Broadway lyric might have expressions that you haven't heard before.

Here is a sample paraphrase of the stanza printed above:

> Wherever a lover needs to go—over earth or sea, or under the earth, or under the waves of the sea, which are obedient to the sea god, or over steep, rocky hills—a lover will succeed in getting to the beloved.

Step 4. *Decide what is the main point* of the poem, the chief message that you want your listeners to get. At this point you personalize the poem and decide what role you are playing when you sing it. Are you singing your own words or someone else's? What is your viewpoint about love in this poem? Are you a philosopher expressing an opinion? Or are you waiting hopefully for someone to find you and fall in love with you? Or are you a lover yourself, and you want everyone to know that you will stop at nothing to win your love?

Step 5. *Read the poem aloud with expression, phrasing, and accentuation.*

- For *expression*, find the words that communicate action and feeling. "Smiles," "revives," and "delight" are energy words.

- Find the *phrasing*, because your breathing will depend on it when you sing. For instance, you will probably connect the first two lines of the poem together and sing them in one breath.

- Notice the correct *accentuation* of the poem because it may give you clues about the musical rhythm.

Step 6. *Listen to the music again and whisper the text in rhythm* with it. Tap three beats to a measure, just as you did while learning the melody. Whispering is recommended so that you can hear and simultaneously practice articulating the consonants of the words.

Let each word have its full time; for instance, in *"Over the mountain . . ."* the second word needs a full beat. Ignore the fact that the beat is broken into two eighth notes.

At this stage several things happen at once: you are practicing rhythms, memorizing the words, learning to articulate them in time, and learning to read ahead, so that your eye is always just ahead of the word you are saying.

Step 7. *Listen to the music and speak the text in rhythm.* Speak with your voice at a little higher pitch than usual because your singing voice is probably even higher. Let your voice sound alive and loving, not low in energy. As you do these steps with all of the stanzas of the song, be patient. Go slowly enough to keep the rhythms clear, accurate, and easy. You are forming vocal habits and breathing habits that will make the song easier when you are ready to sing it.

## Singing the song

When you have mastered the rhythms, the melody, and the words, you are ready for Step 8: *Combine the melody with the words.* You were already singing the melody with nonsense syllables; now you use words instead and adjust the phrasing so that the words continue to make sense.

You can probably sing this song confidently by now, or you soon will be able to. With more difficult songs you might need to repeat some of the steps already done and work things out by yourself. Then you are ready to memorize the song and give all of your attention to expression. When you are ready to share your song with an audience, there are further tips in chapter 9, "Performing a Song."

## Breathing points

When do I breathe? As often as you like, when you are speaking, and people seldom think about it. In singing you take much deeper breaths, but you still want people to think about your song and not about your breathing.

The song we have been studying has rest signs for the breaths. For a singer a rest sign does not mean that nothing happens; it means "breathe."

If a song does not have rest signs where you need them, look for commas and other punctuation and then for ways to group the words for sense. *The words have to make sense.* If you pay attention to word meanings, you will never breathe in the middle of a word or between words that have to connect with each other.

When you know where you want to breathe, just shorten the preceding note and take your breath so that you can begin the next phrase on time. For instance, if you are running out of air before measure 16, there is a comma in measure 14 where you can breathe in after "steep-est." Change the quarter note on "-est" to an eighth note and insert an eighth rest. No rest sign is printed there because some singers don't need or want it.

Sometimes breathing points are indicated in songs with written signs above the staff, either a wedge ( **V** ) or a comma ( **,** ), or with long curved lines called phrase marks. If a song has a second stanza, you may have to discover different phrasing from the first stanza.

### Catch breaths

Some music does not show any rest signs at all, for instance, "The Star-Spangled Banner" on page 100. You are expected to take quick breaths, called **catch breaths,** that do not break the musical rhythm.

It's time to use the skill of taking quick breaths that you learned in exercise 2.6, "Starter." Keeping good posture, let the abdominal muscles relax suddenly; the diaphragm descends quickly and air rushes in. It may take practice, but there is no need to lift your shoulders or do anything else that looks uncomfortable.

Remember that the note *before* the breathing point is shortened. The note *after* the new breath must begin on time and last for its full length.

### Take enough breaths!

Young singers can easily be carried along with momentum so that they forget to breathe at sensible places. A long phrase serves no purpose if it runs through punctuation marks and the words make no sense. A long phrase is not beautiful if the voice sounds tense and unsupported at the end or the singing ends with an emergency gasp.

On the contrary, short phrases can be useful for emphasis and variety. For instance, the third stanza contains parenthetical phrases that might be set off with catch breaths, the phrases "Poor thing, . . ." and "if so you call him, . . ." Experiment with catch breaths at the commas in measures 23, 24, and 30 and see whether you like the effect.

### Exercises

Although this chapter was not about vocal technique, it suggests some exercises to improve the musical quality of our singing. We will work on ear-training, phrasing, and dynamics.

**5.1 Do-Re-Mi Scale.** We all know these syllables from Rodgers and Hammerstein's song "Do-Re-Mi" from *The Sound of Music.* Purpose: to sing long tones with close attention to intonation.

CD 1 Track 18

**5.2  2-Note Sighs.** Connect these pairs of tones smoothly. Purpose: to practice the syllables with clear intonation and easy catch breaths.

Do you sense that the pitches do and ti are closer to each other than the pitches ti-la, la-so, and so-fa? Also that fa and mi are closer to each other than are mi-re and re-do? This may not be immediately clear, but with practice you will realize that do-ti and fa-mi are half-steps and the others are whole steps. Recognizing the half-steps helps us to sing accurately in tune.

CD 1 Track 19

Do,    ti,       ti,    la,       la,    so,       so,    fa,

fa,    mi,       mi,    re,       re,    do,    ti,    do.

**5.3  3-Note Sighs.** Connect these groups of tones smoothly. Purpose: the same as in exercise 5.2

CD 1 Track 20

Do,    ti,    la,       ti,    la,    so,       la,    so,    fa,       so,    fa,    mi,

fa,    mi,    re,       mi,    re,    do,       re,    do,    ti,    do.

**5.4  Swell.** In order to sing expressively you have to be able to sing louder and softer. Begin with just three clear levels, soft (p), medium (mf), and loud (f). Avoid "super-soft" and "super-loud" for now. Purpose: to realize that different volume levels are available throughout the voice.

CD 1 Track 21

_p  mf  f  mf  p_       _p  mf  f  mf  p_       _p  mf  f  mf  p_

Ma-ma-ma-ma - ma,       ma-ma-ma-ma - ma,       ma-ma-ma-ma - ma,

_p  mf  f  mf  p_       _p  mf  f  mf  p_       _p  mf  f  mf  p_

ma-ma-ma-ma - ma,       ma-ma-ma-ma - ma,       ma-ma-ma-ma - ma.

*Additional reading*        *If you want to know more about poetry, you will enjoy this attractive collection:*

*The Classic Hundred: All-Time Favorite Poems,* edited by William Harmon. Columbia University Press, 1990.

ALWAYS Know the meaning of every word you sing.

ALWAYS Focus on the main message you want to get across.

ALWAYS Keep the rhythm of your song alive.

# 6 Vowels and Vocal Color

**Guiding Questions:** *How can I sing so that everyone understands my words?*
*Can I sing the way I speak or do I have to change words to sing them?*
*How can I color my voice so that there is variety in my singing?*

Do you enjoy hearing a language you do not understand? Or are you bored? Hearing a few sentences in an unfamiliar language may be fun, but we usually grow bored with sounds that we can't understand.

That's how people feel when they don't understand the words we sing. They try to catch what they can, but soon their minds wander. They miss a large part of the pleasure that they should get from the song.

Why does this happen? We don't intentionally fail to communicate!

Often, singers don't realize that others are not understanding their words. To sing clearly is definitely more difficult than to speak clearly. Music inevitably alters language sounds, by:

- Stretching short vowels over long notes;
- Giving full length and tone to syllables that might be very weak, or even omitted, in conversational speech;
- Carrying the voice higher than it goes in normal speech (vowels are less distinguishable from each other on higher notes of the female voice).

These problems can be overcome with knowledge, awareness, and thoughtful practice.

## Speaking as a basis for singing

*Singing is, first of all, saying.* This maxim contains one of the keys to moving the emotions of an audience. Your listeners can be persuaded only if they understand what you say.

*If your speaking voice is free and resonant, it furnishes the best foundation and model for singing.* On the other hand, if your speaking voice is not free and resonant—if it is timid, breathy, or dull or if you have an unpleasant regional twang or drawl—then your singing will suffer, too. Be open to the possibility that your speaking voice needs work in order to release the full potential of your singing voice.

What kinds of changes have to be made in moving from clear speaking to clear singing diction? Vowels are lengthened and they must be recognizable and distinct from each other. Consonants must also be stronger. Consonants that we usually stop inside our mouths must be spoken out. Although we want to sing smooth *legato* melodies, we have to articulate words so that they don't run together in ways that obscure meaning.

Unfortunately, many people have not learned to pronounce the English language clearly and beautifully. Most of us have some regional speech habits and pronunciations that are distracting or confusing to people from other areas. People can miss the important things we want to express if they are distracted by our local accents. We need to learn standard American pronunciation, which sounds correct and appropriate to any English-speaking person in the United States or Canada.

## What is diction?

**Diction** is the area of vocal technique related to making words clear. It includes the concepts of **pronunciation,** choosing the correct sounds, and **articulation,** forming the sounds. When we do these things well and add phrasing and expression, we have good diction.

Performers may use both informal and formal styles of diction. If you are going to perform in blue jeans, then your hometown accent will sound fine. If the performance requires dressing up or wearing a costume, then your diction should be "dressed up" also. Let your diction match the style of the occasion and the style of the music.

You don't need to change your everyday speaking voice unless you want to or unless your speech habits are unhealthful. You don't have to give up your familiar way of speaking to learn new techniques for singing.

## Thinking phonetically

Children learn about vowel letters: A, E, I, O, U, and sometimes Y. As singers, we think in terms of *sounds* rather than letters. (From now on this book uses the word "vowel" to mean vowel sound, not letter.) To sing in English we need a minimum of 12 vowel sounds, each one distinct from the others. It is helpful to have an alphabet that has a letter or symbol for each one; luckily one already exists: the **International Phonetic Alphabet (IPA).**

**Phonetics** is the scientific study of speech sounds. Scholars of phonetics developed the IPA so that the sounds of any language can be written down. Each IPA symbol stands for only one sound and no other. With the IPA one can write down, or **transcribe,** the sounds of a word or a whole text. The IPA symbols used for English are useful in studying other languages as well.

IPA is used to show "Standard American" pronunciations in *A Pronouncing Dictionary of American English* by Kenyon and Knott. If you are used to some other pronunciations, just be aware that they are not Standard American and might cause confusion.

All of the IPA symbols used in English are listed in Appendix B, page 300.

### Some customs are observed when writing IPA transcriptions:

- Use a symbol for every sound that can be heard, regardless of how many letters are in the word.
- Do not show silent letters.
- Do not show punctuation.
- Do not use capital letters, even for names, because they may stand for different sounds.
- Enclose IPA symbols in square brackets when they occur in a normal context, as in this example sentence: "The sound [ju] is spelled one way in 'cute' [kjut] and differently in 'pew' [pju]."

# Vowels

Vowels are vocal sounds that are made with a *free, unrestricted flow of breath.* They differ from consonants, which all obstruct the air in one way or another.

When the throat and mouth are the most relaxed, the most like an open tube, the vowel sound that they resonate is Uh [ʌ]. To make other vowels, the lips and tongue change the shape of the mouth and throat resonators. (Voice scientists are not sure whether the vocal folds help to form the vowels because of the difficulty of measuring them while they are in motion.)

We can understand other vowels by the way they differ and how much they differ from Uh. Every vowel can be described as **bright, neutral** or **dark.** Bright vowels, such as Ee, are formed primarily by the tongue; dark vowels, such as Oo, are formed by rounding the lips. Neutral vowels, such as Uh, use little or no shaping by either tongue or lips.

In each category vowels can also be described as being **closed** or **open,** referring to how low the jaw is dropped and to the way the tongue is lifted or not lifted toward the roof of the mouth (palate). No vowel is completely closed and most vowels are more open for singing than for speech.

All vowels *can resonate freely,* and singers train themselves to have a uniform feeling of vibration for all vowels. This sensation differs from speech theory, which often refers to "front vowels," "mid-vowels" and "back vowels." Such terms refer to the part of the tongue that is active in shaping the mouth resonator; it has nothing to do with the vibratory sensations experienced by good singers. This book does not use the term "back vowel" because it might mislead a student into making a throaty tone.

All vowels can be produced with the *tip of the tongue lightly touching the lower teeth.* Most singers find this position helpful for vocal relaxation.

Finally, all vowels *can be prolonged* for as long as the music requires. We speak of long and short vowels, but in singing all vowels can be long.

## Seven Italian vowels

Because Italians were the first to invent opera and to export singing stars to other nations, classical vocal study traditionally emphasizes the Italian language. Some teachers train their students first in Italian because Italian has fewer different vowels than English. For these reasons we highlight the Italian vowels which are numbered below to match the list of IPA symbols on page 300.

The seven Italian vowels are:

| IPA symbol | English name | Some possible spellings |
| --- | --- | --- |
| 1. [i] | Ee | bee, sea, brief, machine |
| 3. [e] | Pure Ay | chaotic, dictates |
| 4. [ɛ] | Open Eh | met, less, head, said |
| 6. [a] | Bright Ah | aisle (British: ask, dance) |
| 9. [ɔ] | Open O (or Aw) | ought, dawn, haul, wall |
| 10. [o] | Pure Oh | hotel, obey |
| 12. [u] | Oo | true, who, moo, few, through |

## Bright vowels

The four bright Italian vowels are differentiated from each other by how high the middle of the tongue rises. The tip of the tongue always rests behind the lower teeth. The lips may either smile or stay relaxed.

1. [i], *Ee,* is the brightest of all vowels and has the least space between the tongue and palate. The tongue rises forward, and the sides of the tongue contact the upper molars. We say "Smile and say cheese," but the smile doesn't affect the vowel.

In singing [i], the mouth space usually needs to be larger than in speaking, but the opening is less than for any other vowel. For acoustical reasons, sopranos may find that a pure [i] is not resonant on their highest notes and that they can substitute [e] on high notes with no loss of clarity.

3. [e], *Pure Ay,* is also a bright vowel. Its degree of openness is about halfway between [i] and [a]. More about this vowel later.

4. [ɛ], *Open Eh,* is bright but more open than [e]. The tongue rises forward, but only a little.

6. [a], *Bright Ah,* the true "Italian ah," is the most open of the Italian vowels. In order to discover it, say the bright vowels in order, opening them gradually: [i, e, ɛ, a]. The tongue is very slightly forward of its resting position.

Standard American pronunciation does not use Bright Ah by itself, although it is used by some British, as well as some Easterners and Southerners. In chapter 8 we will see how important Bright Ah is in diphthongs.

Whenever [a] occurs in British pronunciation, Standard American uses [æ], as in "chaff, laugh, command, branch, nasty, mast." If you ever want to sound British, as in singing songs from *Pirates of Penzance* or *Camelot,* sing [a] instead of [æ] in such words.

## Dark vowels

The three dark Italian vowels are differentiated from each other by how small the lips are rounded. In casual conversation most Americans use little or no lip rounding, so that the tongue takes over the work of forming the dark vowels. Singers and formally trained actors learn to shape dark vowels with the lips and to keep the tongue much more relaxed. The tongue should not pull back for the dark vowels; the tip rests behind the lower teeth.

12. [u], *Oo,* is the darkest of all vowels and has the smallest opening of the rounded lips. Most singers find it easy to sing [u] softly because of its natural darkness, but for projection of a strong tone it may be necessary to open [u] somewhat toward [o]. Think of [u] as a "hollow" sound, with space in the mouth.

10. [o], *Pure Oh,* is a dark vowel, and its degree of openness is about halfway between [a] and [u]. More about this vowel later.

9. [ɔ] *Open O,* is also dark but much more open than [o]. Although it is usually spelled with the letter A, it is more like *Oh* with the jaw lowered.

> Personal note from the author: I grew up with a western Pennsylvania dialect that did not contain Open O, and I had to learn it when I studied singing. Eventually, I used it a lot for vocalizing.
>
> Does your local speech use [ɔ]? Pronounce these pairs of words: "hock" and "hawk"; "la" and "law"; "sod" and "sawed"; "cot" and "caught." The second word in each pair contains [ɔ]. If the paired words sound identical to your ears, you are among those whose speech lacks the [ɔ] sound. Practice saying "hawk," "law," "sawed," and "caught" with your lips rounded in order to get used to this new sound. You don't have to change your daily speech unless you want to, but your singing will benefit from knowing this new vowel.

## Pure Ay and Pure Oh in English

In singing English, Ay and Oh are seldom pure vowels. If you say Ay slowly and listen carefully, you will hear and feel that the vowel sound changes as you end it. And if you say Oh carefully, it will also change at the end. Such combinations of two vowels, called **diphthongs,** are explained in chapter 8.

We nearly always make diphthongs out of Ay and Oh, especially in speaking slowly or in pronouncing strong, stressed syllables. Ay and Oh remain pure only when we speak rapidly or when they are in weak (unstressed) syllables, as in the example words above.

If the pure vowel and the diphthong are so much alike, why do we need to distinguish between them? Because English requires the diphthong and sounds artificial without it, and yet other languages require the pure vowel.

Music slows words down so much that every detail can be heard, and every language has its own distinctive sounds.

In Italian you need all seven vowels described so far: [i, e, ɛ, a, ɔ, o, u].

In church Latin you need these five: [i, ɛ, a, ɔ, u].

In Spanish you need these five: [i, e, a, o, u].

**Eight English vowels**

The remaining vowels are so characteristic of English that they are difficult for most foreigners. Because we learned most of them as "short" vowels in spoken English, we have to focus carefully on their exact quality when they are stretched long by music. We will vocalize on the ones we need and become comfortable with them.

| IPA symbol | English name | Some possible spellings |
|---|---|---|
| 2. [ɪ] | Short I | sing, rely, been, women, busy |
| 5. [æ] | Short A | sang, mash, marry, cat, carry |
| 7. [ɑ] | Dark Ah | father, far, wander, watch |
| 8. [ɒ] | Short O | cot, sorry, hock, gone |
| 11. [ʊ] | Short U | full, put, good, would, woman |
| 13. [ʌ] | Uh | ". . . but young love does flood . . ." |
| 14. [ə] | Schwa | *a* cactus, th*e* nation, |
| 15. [ɜ] | Er | serve, earth, girl, worth, hurt |

2. [ɪ], *Short I*, is a bright vowel, a little more open than [i]. Practice saying [ɪ] with the tongue touching the lower teeth, and then say "shimmy" with the same clear vowel quality. If [ɪ] is sung with the tongue pulled back, as many people do before or after [ɪ], as in "little" or "ill," the beauty and special color of the [ɪ] are lost.

5. [æ], *Short A*, is a bright, open vowel. Some people shy away from the brightness of [æ], but it can be beautiful if the mouth opens freely and the tongue lies forward and relaxed.

[æ] has a bad reputation because it is usually spoken with unnecessary tension and/or nasality. Some singers and choir directors dislike this ugliness so much that they change [æ] to [ɑ], so that "a man's hand" becomes "a mahn's hahnd." This is not a British accent; it is just unclear and confusing. Remember that Shakespeare wrote *Hamlet*, not *Hahmlet*.

7. [ɑ], *Dark Ah*, lies in the center of the vowel color range. It is the most open of all vowels, meaning that the tongue lies quite low in the mouth, with the jaw comfortably open.

Because it is so open, [ɑ] is a favorite for female singers' high notes. It can take on various shades of color, depending on the mood of the song. Individual speakers use a range of colors for this vowel, depending on their regional origin and preference. To find the normal or "real" [ɑ], which is exactly in the center of the color range, alternate [ɑ] with brighter and darker vowels: exercise 6.3 does this.

8. [ɒ], *Short O*, is recognized by some speech texts, but when it is lengthened by music, it sounds just like [ɑ]. Instead of vocalizing on [ɒ], we will sing [ɑ] instead.

11. [ʊ], *Short U*, the second darkest vowel, after [u], is only slightly more open than [u]. Practice it as you do [u], with your tongue touching the lower teeth and a feeling of hollowness in your mouth. Unlike [ɒ], this vowel keeps its quality even in singing.

13. [ʌ], *Uh*, or "Ugh" if you prefer, is a moderately open neutral vowel. If someone hits you suddenly in the abdomen, this might be the sound that comes out. It is so fully relaxed and free that some singers habitually sing [ɒ] when they mean to sing [ʌ]. Many vocal exercises in this book use this relaxed vowel.

14. [ə], *Schwa*, is always short and always weak (unstressed). It is a neutral vowel, a little less open than [ʌ]. A schwa changes according to its neighbors: it is brighter in a happy mood or next to bright vowels, but it is darker in a somber mood or next to dark vowels. It is more open if it occurs between open vowels, more closed between closed vowels.

When we lengthen [ə] for singing, it usually sounds most like vowel 13 [ʌ]. If we were asked to vocalize a phrase on a schwa, we would use [ʌ].

Despite its weakness, [ə] deserves special study because contrast between strong and weak syllables is characteristic of English. In some languages (French and Japanese, for instance) all syllables have equal strength, but not in English. A singer who ignores this fact and sings all syllables with equal strength sounds laborious and monotonous.

Schwas occur often. Slowly say this sentence aloud; each word contains one schwa: "The handsome captain salutes a respected woman." Did you notice how many different ways the schwa sound is spelled?

The name "schwa" comes from a Hebrew alphabet sign, *shva*, which usually indicates a weak vowel just like ours. Sometimes it shows that there is no vowel where one might be expected. English also has words in which we see a vowel letter but leave it out in pronunciation as well as words in which no vowel is written but one must be sung. Here are some examples transcribed into IPA to show how they must be sung.

|  | Said: | Should be sung: |
| --- | --- | --- |
| cotton | [kɑtn] | [kɑtən] |
| bottom | [bɑtm] | [bɑtəm] |
| little | [lɪtl] | [lɪtəl] |
| didn't | [dɪdnt] | [dɪdənt] |

In chapter 8 you will learn more about [ə] and its role in a family of schwa-diphthongs.

15. [ɜ], *Er*, is also a neutral vowel, like vowels 13 and 14, but it is less open and somewhat darkened. There is always an R in the spelling. When most people hear this sound, they are more aware of the R than of the vowel.

To sing [ɜ] beautifully, let your lips round slightly. With your tongue lying low and forward in your mouth, the middle of the tongue rises a little. Above all, avoid bunching up the back of your tongue as many people do when saying [r].

[ɜ] is another vowel that has a bad reputation because so many people pronounce it with tension and an ugly tone. An angry dog says "Grr," and some people go almost that far with this vowel.

Practice saying "earth" and "hers" with no [r] at all. When sung well, this vowel is practically identical with the French vowel in *jeune* and the German vowel in *könnte*. Once found, [ɜ] is an easy vowel for most voices to vocalize.

**Summary of fifteen vowels**

Vowels 1–6, [i, ɪ, e, ɛ, æ, a] are all bright vowels, which require the tongue to lift and move forward. Use either smiling or relaxed lips.

Vowels 8–12 [ɑ, ɔ, o, ʊ, u] are all darkened by rounding the lips. Let the tongue remain low and relaxed.

Vowels 7 and 13–15 [a, ʌ, ə, ɜ] are all neutral vowels that allow great variety of coloration according to mood.

**Equalizing the vowels**

Almost everyone finds some vowels easier and stronger than others; our goal in exercising is to sing all vowels with equal comfort and strong resonance while we also give each vowel its own special sound.

For the sake of evenness in singing, let your mouth open moderately for all vowels. Open vowels are likely to be naturally louder than closed vowels. Avoid over-opening the naturally open vowels [æ, ɑ]. Open up the closed vowels [i, ɪ, u, ʊ] more than would seem right for their pure quality. Practice all vowels in relation to the most neutral one, Uh [ʌ].

Also for evenness, avoid exaggerated mouth positions, such as grinning. Once you understand the various vowel colors, form them as easily as possible.

**Vocalizing on English vowels**

There are some English vowel sounds that we do not vocalize, because in singing:

- [a] always changes into either [æ] or [ɑ];
- [ɒ] changes to [ɑ] when sustained; and
- [ə] changes to [ʌ] when sustained.

We will put off vocalizing vowel 3 [e] and vowel 10 [o] until we study them as diphthongs in chapter 8.

For the ten remaining vowels our basic exercise method is to compare and contrast them in groups of two or three. Help others and ask them to help you in learning how to distinguish the vowels clearly.

From this point onward, our vocal exercises will use IPA symbols, except when whole English words are used. The consonants used here are pronounced with normal English sounds.

**Coloring your voice for expression**

As babies, we learned that bright vocal colors go with a smiling face and that dark vocal colors go with a scowling face. Unconsciously adult listeners also sense a relationship between facial expressions and vocal sounds.

Bright vowels sung with a smiling face enhance the sound of a happy song. For a more somber mood, the bright vowels can be sung with the lips relaxed. If your higher tones have a bright, edgy quality, or if you to want add a soothing quality to words such as "peace" or "sleep," you can reduce the brightness of [i] by rounding your lips in the direction of [u].

Dark vowels sung with rounded lips bring out the mood of a serious song. For a happier mood, or if listeners say that your vocal quality is too dark, you can practice singing dark vowels with a smile, as in "joke."

Besides these basic examples of vocal coloring, words and tones can be colored in many more subtle ways. Imagination is our principal tool.

**Exercises**

6.1 **Bright Vowels.** Sing smoothly, with clear vowel qualities and even dynamics. These vowels are in the words "me, muss, miss, mess, mat." Purpose: to establish the bright vowels and to compare each one with [ʌ].

CD 1 Track 22

**6.2 Dark Vowels.** Sing smoothly, just as in the last exercise. These vowels are in the words "do, good, law." Purpose: to establish the dark vowels and to compare each one with [ʌ].

CD 1 Track 23

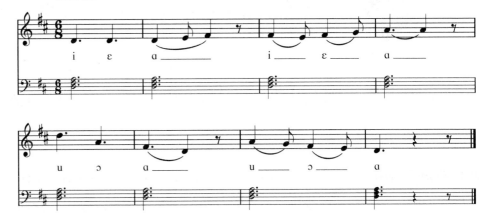

**6.3 Row with Ah.** Bright vowels tend to brighten other nearby sounds, and dark vowels tend to darken other nearby sounds. Purpose: by singing Ah after bright sounds and then after dark ones, we can find a medium sound for Ah.

CD 1 Track 24

**6.4 Nonsense waltz.** Sing smoothly. For fun, put emotions into these nonsense words, singing as if you were angry, jealous, giddy, etc. Purpose: to establish *legato* singing in vowels that English and Italian have in common.

CD 1 Track 25

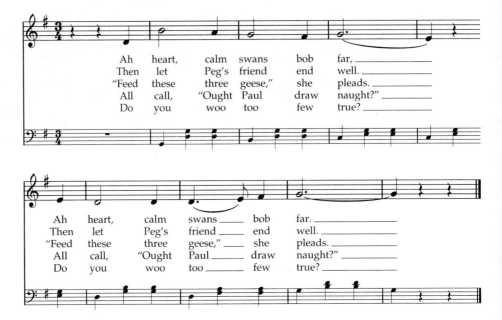

**6.5 Tri-puh-lets.** Avoid any sound of consonant *r* in the second syllable. Purpose: to establish [3] as a singable vowel with no consonant character.

mɑ _____ m3 _____ mɑ     mɑ _____ m3 _____ mɑ
si _____ s3 _____ si        si _____ s3 _____ si
bu _____ b3 _____ bu      bu _____ b3 _____ bu

**6.6 Vowel Cousins.** The following pairs of vowels have the same degree of opening. They help to "tune" each other; in other words, improvement in one vowel also leads to improvement in the other one.

i __ u __ i    u __ i __ u    i __ u __ i    u __ i __ u
ɪ __ ʊ __ ɪ    ʊ __ ɪ __ ʊ    ɪ __ ʊ __ ɪ    ʊ __ ɪ __ ʊ
ɛ __ ɔ __ ɛ    ɔ __ ɛ __ ɔ    ɛ __ ɔ __ ɛ    ɔ __ ɛ __ ɔ
æ __ ʌ __ æ    ʌ __ æ __ ʌ    æ __ ʌ __ æ    ʌ __ æ __ ʌ

***Additional reading***

*For clear, humorous, and thorough instruction about singing words clearly:*

*The Singer's Manual of English Diction* by Madeleine Marshall. Schirmer Books, 1953.

*Singers, actors, and broadcasters rely on the Standard American pronunciations in:*

*A Pronouncing Dictionary of American English* by John S. Kenyon and Thomas A. Knott. G. & C. Merriam Co., 1953.

ALWAYS Think the vowel sound before you sing it and continue thinking it while you sustain the tone.

ALWAYS Rest the tip of the tongue against the lower front teeth for all vowels.

# 7

# Consonants and Clarity

*Guiding Questions:*      ***How important are consonants?***
***When I sing, will consonants help or get in the way?***
***What if several consonants come together? Will they make my singing sound choppy?***

COMMON courtesy tells us to speak so that others can understand us. We have learned not to mumble or shout; we speak as clearly as we need to without exaggerating. We will try to sing just that clearly, with the difference that we may want to sing in a large room for many people. Many singers energize their vocal tone and forget to energize their consonants. If your singing tone becomes strong enough to hear 100 feet away, then the consonants need to be reinforced to carry across the same distance. Some consonants carry almost as strongly as vowel tones, but others are weak and must be exaggerated in order to be heard.

Aside from clear diction, some consonants actually help us to improve tone and clarify vowel quality. That's why we have already done vocalises that include consonant sounds.

## Semivowels

Standard American has two sounds that resemble vowels in that they are "made with an unrestricted flow of breath," but they function as consonants because they always precede other vowels. They are called **semivowels** or **semiconsonants.** They are also called **glides** because the articulators move while saying them. They are numbered in the list below the same as in the list of IPA symbols on page 300.

| IPA symbol | English name | Some possible spellings |
|---|---|---|
| 16. [j] | Yah | you, yes, unit, few, Europe |
| 17. [w] | Wah | water, weed, wail, whoa!, one |

**16.** [j], *Yah*, begins from an [i] position, with the tongue lifted forward. Say "you" in slow motion, slowly enough to hear the sound of [i] as you begin and the change that occurs as your tongue moves from [i] to [u], the main vowel of "you."

Notice that U and EW sometimes have the sound of [ju], even though no letter is present to represent the semivowel. There also is a large group of words in which [j] is optional for everyday speech, but required for "dress-up" speech. (Do you remember the distinction we made between "blue jeans" singing and "dress-up" singing?) The following pronunciations may sound peculiar to you, but they are appropriate for formal singing.

| Spelling | IPA | Examples |
|----------|-----|----------|
| *du, dew* | [dju] | due, dew, endure, duke |
| *lu* | [lju] | lute, allure (but not if a consonant precedes "l," as in "flute" or "blue") |
| *nu, new* | [nju] | new, news, nude, inure |
| *su, sew* | [sju] | suit, sewer, sue (but not "Susan") |
| | [zju] | resume |
| *tu* | [tju] | tune, Tuesday, student, stupid |
| *th* | [θju] | enthusiasm |

**17.** [w], *Wah*, begins from a [u] position, with rounded lips. Say "we" in slow motion, slowly enough to hear the sound of [u] as you begin and the change that occurs as your tongue moves from [u] to [i], the main vowel.

When you sing a word that starts with a semivowel, be sure that it starts on pitch. If it starts below the pitch and slides up, it sounds lazy and careless.

## Consonants

What all consonants have in common is that they interfere with our breath flow in some way and to some degree. The interference can occur at one of these locations:

- At the lips;
- Between the lower lip and the upper teeth;
- Between the tongue and the teeth;
- Between the tongue and the ridge behind the teeth (called the gum ridge); or
- Between the tongue and the hard palate.

The lips, teeth, tongue, and palate are called **articulators** because of their role in forming consonants.

Every consonant sound is either **voiced,** meaning that the vocal folds vibrate during the sound, or **voiceless,** meaning that they do not. If they are vibrating, then the consonant has a musical pitch. If they are not vibrating, then the consonant is a noise that has no definite musical pitch.

You can check whether a consonant is voiced by feeling your larynx while you say it. Or stop one ear with a finger so that you hear the vibrations that come up from the vocal folds to your inner ear.

An easy one to test is [s], which is merely a noise and sounds the same with your ear stopped or open. Contrast it with [z]; the buzzing sensation that comes from your vocal folds is very noticeable when you feel your larynx or stop an ear.

Check every consonant as you read about it and decide whether it is voiced or voiceless. Voiced consonants, just like vowels and semivowels, must be kept on pitch and not allowed to slide up from below.

Most IPA symbols for consonants are the same as normal alphabet letters. When you have learned the few new ones that are needed, you will be able to write whole words in IPA.

## Hums

We have three "hums," all voiced. They are different from other consonants because breath moves only through the nose rather than the mouth.

| IPA symbol | English name | Some possible spellings |
|------------|--------------|-------------------------|
| 18. [m] | Em | ma, summer, rim |
| 19. [n] | En | now, inner, ban |
| 20. [ŋ] | Ing | singer, finger, angry, anchor |

Test each hum sound. Which one blocks the breath at the lips? At the gum ridge? Farther back on the palate?

Hums are useful to warm up the voice quietly. Hum with an even but economical flow of breath. If your hum sounds breathy, the vocal folds are not working efficiently. Stopping one ear with a finger, you can easily check your tone both for evenness and for clarity. Hums are so much like vowels that some teachers recommend making them last at least twice as long in singing as they do in speech.

At the end of a word many Westerners confuse Ing with Een. Words like "sing" should rhyme with "king" and not with "queen." All hums should end with a clean release and no extra vowel sound.

## Voiced and voiceless pairs

Most English consonants have partners: that is, a voiceless consonant and a voiced one are produced by the same articulators in the same way. For instance, in the list below [f] and [v] are produced in exactly the same way except that [f] is voiceless and [v] is voiced.

Numbers 25–32 are **continuant** consonants, which can be prolonged easily. Numbers 33–40 are all **stop** consonants; they momentarily stop the flow of air.

| IPA symbol | English name | Some possible spellings |
|---|---|---|
| 25. [f] | Eff | fa, often, phrase, laugh |
| 26. [v] | Vee | vigor, over, verve |
| 27. [θ] | Theta | thin, Cathy, path |
| 28. [ð] | Edh | this, either, without, smooth |
| 29. [s] | Ess | solo, essence, kiss, science |
| 30. [z] | Zee | zoo, hazard, present, has |
| 31. [ʃ] | Shah | show, social, nation, sure |
| 32. [ʒ] | Zsa-Zsa | azure, pleasure, massage |
| 33. [p] | Pee | peach, upper, cup |
| 34. [b] | Bee | beach, baby, cub |
| 35. [t] | Tee | teach, atom, cut |
| 36. [d] | Dee | do, odor, head |
| 37. [k] | Kay | keep, tack, calm, accurate |
| 38. [g] | Hard Gee | go, again, tag |
| 39. [tʃ] | Cha-Cha | church, achieve |
| 40. [dʒ] | Soft Gee | gem, jelly, ridge, rajah |

Consonants vary in carrying power from [s], which can be clearly heard even in the softest whisper, to [p], the weakest of all consonants. For public speaking or singing, voiceless consonants often need an extra burst of air, called an **aspiration.** This is what conductors mean when they say, "Spit out your consonants!" Unfortunately, that command often causes choral singers to use more facial tension instead of using more breath.

A special word about the six stops, 33–38: a stop at the end of a word may not be heard unless we add an extra sound. For instance, if you end a word like "sleep" with your lips closed, the word hardly sounds different from "sleet" or "sleek."

For a voiceless final [p], [t], or [k], add aspiration. Practice "sap, sat, sack" with a small burst of air after each final consonant. You can mark final voiceless stops this way: "sap[h]."

The voiced finals [b], [d], and [g] all need a weak schwa for carrying power on the release. Practice singing "rib, rid, rig" with a weak vowel after each final consonant—on pitch, of course! (Hum consonants do not need this extra sound if they are well resonated.) You can mark final voiced stops this way: "beg[ə]."

Just like vowels, voiced consonants must begin and end on pitch, without a glottal attack or any extra sound afterward, except for the special case of final [b], [d], and [g].

## Special consonants

There are some remaining consonants that do not fit the pattern of voiced-voiceless partners.

| IPA symbol | English name | Some possible spellings |
|---|---|---|
| 21. [l] | El | la, follow, sill |
| 22. [r] | Ahr | rib, arrow, far |
| 23. [h] | Aitch | hum, aha! |
| 24. [hw] | Which | what whale? |

**21.** [l], *El*, is made when the pointed tip of the tongue lightly and quickly touches the upper teeth or gum ridge and sound comes around the sides of the tongue. Singers like to vocalize on "la-la-la" because only the tip of the tongue is involved. If [l] is incorrectly curled back along the hard palate, the vowels before and after it are darkened. Correct this by singing "lee-lee-lee" with the tongue pointed forward.

Be aware that a vowel before L stays open and resonant. If the tongue rises too soon or too slowly toward the [l] position, the vowel quality may be spoiled.

**23.** [h], *Aitch*, is a sound of friction as air passes through the open mouth. Let the friction take place high and forward on the roof of the mouth. [h] is a quiet consonant which needs extra energy in a large room.

**24.** [hw], *Which*, is a sound of friction as air passes through lips shaped for [u]. We do not hear the [u] because the lips move quickly to the position of the following vowel. The double symbol, [hw], shows that the sound is frictional, like [h], and also involves a quick semivowel, like [w].

## R: the variable sound

We learned in chapter 6 about the vowel [ɜ], which always has the letter R in its spelling. That is just one of several sounds associated with R.

When R is followed by a vowel, it works as a consonant and must be pronounced. This is true when R and the following vowel are in the same word, as in "rose," and also when they are in different words, as in "far away."

There are two correct ways to pronounce [r] in singing English:

1. *American R* [r], pronounced with the tongue forward, not pulled back or tense. The lips may be rounded. Some experts analyze [r] as a glide, produced by moving from the sound of ɜ to another vowel sound.

2. *Flipped R* [ɾ], if you are using a formal or British style and if the R is between two vowels. To discover this sound, say "veddy meddy" several times quickly, lightening the *dd* until you are saying "very merry."

Caution: Do not *roll* [r]. Rolled R is not part of Standard American.

What if R is followed by a consonant or by a silence? Minimize the Ahr and keep the preceding vowel as relaxed as possible. Sometimes you might omit Ahr completely, so that "lark" is pronounced "lahk." At other times you may sing a schwa instead of Ahr; chapter 8 will tell more about this substitution.

Sometimes a vowel before R is spoiled if the tongue rises too soon or too slowly toward the [r] position. This is such a common fault that almost every voice student has to work on it.

In summary:

- Standard American may use two kinds of *r*: American and Flipped.
- European languages require two kinds of *r*: Rolled and Flipped.

- Ahr before a vowel must be pronounced.
- Ahr before a consonant or a silence is minimized.

## Clusters and legato singing

Our language is rich in consonants. Think of an ordinary sentence like "This plant sprouts from seeds," which has five vowels and seventeen consonant sounds. Between the vowel in "plant" and the vowel in "sprouts" there are five consecutive consonants, three of which are voiceless. No wonder it is difficult to sing smoothly in English!

Some singers become so intent on singing smoothly—the Italian word is *legato*—that they leave out consonants altogether or they articulate them weakly and drown them in a flood of vowel sound. Such singing has no gaps in the sound but unfortunate gaps in the meaning of the words. Listeners catch a bit of text here and there and struggle to guess what the song is about. They are likely to go home saying, "I don't like to hear singers much. You can never understand them." We do not want that to happen!

No book can give separate exercises for all of the thousands of combinations of two, three, four, and five consonants that occur in English. We can, however, work for clarity and agility with tongue twisters and rapid speech patterns.

There are two common problems in diction: weakness, or lack of clarity; and choppiness, or lack of smooth connections. Here are ways to work on and overcome these problems.

If your consonants are too weak, try whispering the words of your song loudly enough so that your whisper can be heard across the room. Notice the energy level that vigorous articulation requires, and then use this level in your singing. Loud whispering is fairly strenuous; do it only for short periods of time.

If your diction is choppy, try chanting, that is, singing the words on a single pitch. At first, let the timing be free so that you can concentrate on the clarity of the vowels and consonants. Pay special attention to the way one word connects to another. Let the final consonant of one word connect with the beginning of the next word, unless your ear tells you that the words have to be separated to make sense. When your chanting is smooth, try doing it in the correct rhythm of the song. Let the legato you have developed carry over into your singing.

## Speaking exercises

Speak these words quickly and lightly in a galloping, singsong rhythm. Let the speed increase until you can speak all four lines in one breath. Purpose: to sensitize the main articulators and develop agility.

> The lips, the teeth, the tip of the tongue,
> the lips, the teeth, the tip of the tongue,
> the lips, the teeth, the tip of the tongue,
> the tip of the, tip of the, tip of the tongue!

Tongue twisters and many poems make excellent articulation drills. Learn to speak the following rapidly and clearly, and then sing them on comfortable middle to low pitches.

> A tutor who tooted a flute
> Once tutored two tooters to toot.
> Said the two to the tutor
> "Is it harder to toot,
> Or to tutor two tooters to toot?"

> Peter Piper picked a peck of pickled peppers. A peck of pickled peppers Peter Piper picked. If Peter Piper picked a peck of pickled peppers, where's the peck of pickled peppers Peter Piper picked?

Blow, bugle, blow, set the wild echoes flying,
Blow, bugle; answer, echoes, dying, dying, dying.
— Alfred Lord Tennyson, from "The Princess"

Boot, saddle, to horse, and away!
Rescue my castle before the hot day
Brightens to blue from its silvery gray.
Boot, saddle, to horse, and away!
— Robert Browning, from "Boot and Saddle"

Because of its meaning, this poem by Emily Dickinson must be spoken slowly but with perfectly precise articulation.

I stepped from plank to plank
A slow and cautious way;
The stars about my head I felt,
About my feet the sea.
I knew not but the next
Would be my final inch,
This gave me that precarious gait
Some call experience.

## Singing exercises

**7.1 La-Beh-Da.** Sing these syllables one measure at a time until you are used to them, then let the speed increase until you can sing all three measures in one breath. (These syllables alternate lip and tongue consonants. Singers have used them since the 1700s.) Purpose: to develop articulatory agility on a musical pattern.

CD 1 Track 28

[la bɛ da mɛ ni pɔ tu la    bɛ da mɛ ni pɔ tu la bɛ    da mɛ ni pɔ tu la bɛ da    mɛ]

**7.2 Connections.** Use these words to test yourself on some of the common problems mentioned in the chapter. Purpose: to exercise consonant connections and consonants that are often misused.

CD 1 Track 29

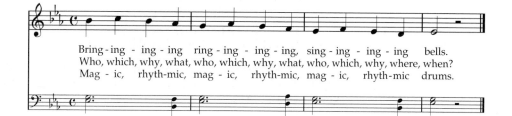

Bring-ing - ing-ing    ring-ing - ing-ing,    sing-ing - ing-ing    bells.
Who, which, why, what, who, which, why, what, who, which, why, where, when?
Mag - ic,    rhyth-mic,    mag - ic,    rhyth-mic,    mag - ic,    rhyth-mic    drums.

**7.3 Yah-Yah.** Sing this pattern with many different consonants and vowels. Be sure that voiced consonants begin on pitch and that the lowest note is in tune. This works well with a teacher or student leading and the class echoing back. Purpose: to ensure that all vowels, semivowels, and voiced and voiceless consonants can be sung both high and low in the voice.

CD 1 Track 30

*Additional reading*    *Audio cassettes with examples spoken by both a female and a male trained speaker accompany this thorough book, which is especially recommended if you would like to lose an accent:*

*American Diction for Singers* by Geoffrey G. Forward. Alfred Publishing Co., Inc., 2001.

ALWAYS Put as much energy into consonants as if you were whispering them.

ALWAYS Keep your jaw muscles relaxed.
(They have nothing to do with articulating vowels and consonants.)

# Double and Triple Vowels

**Guiding Questions:**   *How does one sing syllables with more than one vowel?*
*What about final r?*

WHEN words are slowed down by singing them, we discover surprising things about spelling and pronunciation. Sometimes two letters are pronounced as one sound, while at other times one letter stands for two sounds. Also, some common "vowels" are not single vowels at all but combinations of two or three vowels.

In chapter 6 we noticed that Ay and Oh, when they are spoken slowly, consist of combinations of vowel sounds. Such combinations are called **diphthongs** and **triphthongs,** Greek words that mean "double sounds" and "triple sounds." (Pronounce the "ph" carefully as [f] in both dif-thong and trif-thong.)

Most languages spell out diphthongs clearly with one letter for each vowel. English spelling sneaks diphthongs in without showing them: the phrase "I go" appears to have two vowels in it, but actually it has two diphthongs, adding up to four vowels. Some say that English has no pure vowels, but that is not true either.

As singers, we know that our words will be prolonged by music and that every detail of our pronunciation will be noticeable to our audience. How will we sing "I go" if the music makes each syllable last for several seconds?

## Five common diphthongs

All English diphthongs follow this pattern: *the first vowel is stronger and more open, and the second vowel is weaker and more closed.* (If the weaker vowel comes first, we call it a semivowel, as in the syllables "you" [ju] or "we" [wi].)

The strong/weak vowel pattern leads to our main rule for singing diphthongs: *stay on the stronger vowel as long as possible and sing the weaker vowel as late and as quickly as possible.* Some authorities call the second vowel of a diphthong a "vanish vowel."

The key to singing diphthongs well is knowing exactly what vowel sounds you wish to sing. Some of us speak local dialects that close the vowels more than necessary; singing is more comfortable and pleasant with correct Standard American diphthongs.

Each of the five common diphthongs can be identified by the numbers of the two vowels that make it up. (The numbers come from Appendix B, page 300.)

| IPA symbol | English name | Some possible spellings |
|---|---|---|
| 4+2. [ɛɪ] | Long Ay | late, may, raise, weigh |
| 6+2. [aɪ] | Long I | I, pie, my, aisle |
| 9+2. [ɔɪ] | Oy | toy, noise |
| 6+11. [aʊ] | Ow | how, house |
| 10+11. [oʊ] | Long Oh | so, low, moan |

**4+2.** [ɛɪ], *Long Ay,* is usually described as a combination of vowels 3+1, [ei]. In singing, this combination turns out to be too tense for comfort, and it can be misunderstood as [i]. The sound is better and clearer if we use 4+2, [ɛɪ], prolonging [ɛ] as the main vowel. In order to relax this sound and clarify it in your mind, practice "late" and other Ay words as shown in exercise 8.1. Prolonging [ɛ] may seem peculiar in speaking, but it will be just right when you sing it.

**6+2.** [aɪ], *Long I,* consists of Bright Ah and Short I in Standard American, producing a clear but relaxed pronunciation. For a country-western sound, try changing the second vowel to [i] and spend extra time on it.

**9+2.** [ɔɪ], *Oy,* uses Open Oh and Short I. Even if your local dialect does not use Open Oh as a single vowel, you probably use it in this diphthong.

**6+11.** [aʊ], *Ow,* consists of Bright Ah and Short U. Just as [i] is too closed for good singing of diphthongs, so is [u], and we use [ʊ] instead for the vanish vowel.

**10+11.** [oʊ], *Long Oh,* consists of Pure Oh and Short U. Be sure that the first vowel is a clear Oh; some British dialects use a mixed vowel much like #15, [ɜ], with no Oh quality at all.

## Schwa-diphthongs

We learned in chapter 7 that [r] causes problems if it involves too much tension in the tongue. For greater relaxation, or for very formal English, you may drop *r* completely before another consonant or before a silence. If you do so, you will discover some words in which you can replace [r] with [ə].

Here is an example: "or." In daily speech most Americans say a vowel plus a consonant, [ɔr]. If you want to avoid American *r* and its tongue tension, you can say [ɔə]. It will sound formal, but clear and relaxed. To sound less formal, you can put some [r] coloring into the schwa, saying [ɔɚ]. The hook on the schwa shows that [r] coloring is heard, but it does not completely cover up the vowel quality of the schwa.

There are five such diphthongs in which a schwa replaces a final *r* or *re.* All of them can be spoken with or without [r] coloring. Because [r] coloring is normal and correct in Standard American, we show it in IPA by adding a tag to the schwa.

Remember to relax your tongue when practicing schwa-diphthongs.

| IPA symbol | English name | Some possible spellings |
|---|---|---|
| 2+14. [ɪɚ] | Ear-diphthong | beer, bier, shear, we're, merely |
| 4+14. [ɛɚ] | Air-diphthong | bear, there, their, e'er, careful |
| 7+14. [ɑɚ] | Are-diphthong | far, art, barge, sergeant |
| 9+14. [ɔɚ] | Or-diphthong | shore, soar, your, door, o'er |
| 11+14. [ʊɚ] | Tour-diphthong | cure, poor, your, you're |

Practice these diphthongs just as you do the five main diphthongs. Make the first vowel sound clear, even if the spelling looks confusing. You can try more or less [r] coloring, from none at all to a country twang.

Keep in mind that schwa-diphthongs occur only at times when *r* can be omitted, that is, before a consonant or before a silence (for instance, when you take a breath). If *r* comes before a vowel, the consonant [r] must be pronounced, and there is no schwa-diphthong. Some examples:

- hear it [hɪrɪt]
- swear it [swɛrɪt]
- pour it [pɔrɪt]
- assure it [əʃʊrɪt]

- hereafter [hɪræftɚ]
- wherever [hwɛrɛvɚ]
- forever [fɔrɛvɚ]
- curable [kjʊrəbəl]

## Schwa-triphthongs

If a final [r] sound comes after a diphthong, changing [r] to a schwa or an R-colored schwa results in a triphthong. After practicing the schwa-diphthongs you will have no trouble with these sounds.

| IPA symbol | English name | Some possible spellings |
|---|---|---|
| 6+2+14. [aɪɚ] | Ire-triphthong | fire, briar, lyre, choir |
| 6+11+14. [aʊɚ] | Our-triphthong | sour, flower |

In both triphthongs [a] is prolonged in singing; the two weaker vowels come quickly and lightly at the end. Again, if the next sound is a vowel, the *r* must be pronounced, and there is no schwa.

Our goal in learning about schwa-diphthongs and schwa-triphthongs is to reduce the amount of tongue tension associated with R. We usually think that formality means stiffness, but in this case formal speech brings ease and relaxation in using the tongue.

## Exercises

**8.1 Diphthongs.** Practice this pattern with many different words that contain diphthongs. These words are written in IPA; what are they? Purpose: to identify the vowels that must be lengthened in the five main diphthongs.

CD 1 Track 31

**8.2 Diphthong and Triphthong Slurs.** Purpose: to identify the components of the schwa-diphthongs.

CD 1 Track 32

ALWAYS Sing a clear, pure vowel for most of the length of a diphthong.
(It will be clear only if your idea of it is clear.)

# Performing a Song

**Guiding Questions:**   *How can I get the most feeling out of a song: is there a "right way," or can I do it all my own way?*
*What is "style"?*
*How can I keep a song interesting from beginning to end?*
*What is the role of my accompanist?*
*How can I get over stage fright?*
*How should I behave on stage, and how can I get the meaning of a song across to an audience?*

Y OU have been learning about the technique of singing: how your voice works and how to sing so that your voice sounds its best and does what you want it to do. It is time now to sing songs, while you continue to learn.

Should you wait to sing songs until your voice is "perfect"? No. In fact, your vocal technique develops more quickly if you combine working on technique and working on songs. You will draw inspiration from the emotional energy of a song you love. Also, your voice learns to work comfortably and reliably when you sing the same music many times, staying alert to the goals of beautiful tone and physical ease.

The goal of your work is to sing songs for others. When that time comes, you must be able to focus on the words and music of the song and trust that the good vocal habits you have practiced will keep you singing well.

## Interpretation

Notes printed on a page—we call them music, but there really is no music until we make the sounds that they stand for. Everything that the songwriter or composer wants to say has to come through the performer, and every performer makes an individual contribution to the way the music sounds. In most classical music a good musician tries to perform with personal emotion and imagination and yet be as faithful as possible to what the composer imagined. In some other styles the performer is expected to use the written notes as a starting point and create a more individualized statement.

**Interpretation** is what we do in the psychological and aesthetic areas of music. Just as your speaking voice and inflections are personal to you, your performance of a piece of music is inevitably different from anyone else's.

What follows are some basic principles to guide you in discovering your own interpretations of your songs.

## Working with the words

*The words come first.* Words are written before music, nearly always. The composer takes the feelings in the words and puts them into music. We re-discover those feelings and let them guide our singing. To interpret a song well, we have to understand the words and feel good about putting them across to other people. They determine many things about how we perform, including when we breathe and our facial expression. Everything we do must fit the words and never go against them.

> "Words make you think thoughts. Music makes you feel a feeling. But a song makes you feel a thought."
>
> E. Y. Harburg, lyricist of "Over the Rainbow"

Good song texts are full of words and ideas to spark your imagination. Once you understand every word and phrase of the text, there will still be questions you need to answer for yourself:

- Are you presenting your own personal thoughts, or playing a role? What role?
- Did something just happen before the song that makes you sing it? What?
- In your imagination, are you at some particular place or time? Where and when?
- How calm or excited are you, and in what way? (Preferably, *very* excited!)
- What is the main idea that you want to get across? Or what do you want to do or have someone else do at the end of the song?

Searching for the answers to these questions and others like them will help you to bring out the most that is in the song. This is what professional actors do, and you can do it, too.

## Working with the music

*Rhythm is the heartbeat of music,* as we all know from intuition and experience. If the rhythm is weak or unsteady, so is the music. Even knowing this, young singers often are so concerned about vocal quality and other aspects of music that they let the rhythm waver or stop altogether.

There are two rhythmic principles that will keep you from "losing the beat." First, *the rhythm starts with the first note of music and continues until the last note dies away.* If there is a piano introduction, start singing mentally with the first note you hear. If there are interludes in the song, sing through them mentally, and also through a postlude after the song. If your mind wanders during the music, the listeners' minds will wander, too, even if they don't know why. Whenever you are not singing, keep listening to the piano and enjoying the music. Your enjoyment will show, and the audience will pay attention too.

Second, *you may hurry or slow down any note of music at any time for any interpretive reason.* You have complete freedom—and complete responsibility. The basic beat of the music, the tempo, may quicken in order to express excitement. Much more often the tempo slows down in order to focus expression on a certain note or series of notes or to express some degree of relaxation or satisfaction or some other feeling. No rule tells us exactly when and how much to vary tempos; our imaginations must tell us.

## Musical styles

Every singer performs in an individual way, but the best singers have a sense of "style." They understand both the style that is contained in the song and how that interacts with their own personal style.

"Style" means many things in musical performance. Here are some of the ways musicians talk about style. Try to relate these to actual pieces of music and singers you have heard. Style can mean:

- A type of music: classical music in contrast to pop music, R&B in contrast to country;
- A historical period: Classical music in contrast to Baroque music, which came before it, and Romantic music, which came after it;
- A manner of expression: dramatic in contrast to lyrical;
- A way of performing that we associate with a specific composer or school of composers, such as Mozart's style or a Russian style;
- A way of performing that belongs to an individual.

How do you learn about style? By listening thoughtfully to many kinds of music, done by many kinds of performers. Reading about music and musicians will help you build a vocabulary and define your ideas about styles. Through listening, reading, discussion, and experimentation you will learn what musical styles you like best, what styles you most want to perform, and how to develop a personal style.

Your personal style emerges as your individual vocal quality develops and as you recognize and emphasize the things you do best. You will always be influenced by other singers you hear, so it is important to hear the best. Listen and learn from many singers so that you are not trapped by imitating just one. As you develop your personal style, you learn to eliminate sounds that imitate others and use sounds that are yours alone.

## Beginning, middle, and end

Because we cannot see music as it goes by us in time, we often talk about it in words that describe shapes. **Form** is one such word, and it describes patterns of repetition or nonrepetition in music. Understanding the form of a song makes it easier to memorize. More important, awareness of musical form helps you to perform better. If we understand the form ourselves, we can help the audience to know when a song repeats, where the climax is, and when the end is coming.

## Strophic songs

Many songs are written in **stanzas,** or verses, using the same music two or more times to different words. Such songs are called **strophic,** a word derived from Greek for "a turning," because a singer would usually turn from one side of the audience to the other at the end of a stanza (still a good idea!).

A good melody is worth hearing more than once, and the audience will remain interested if we keep the words interesting. The last stanza might need something special to give it a sense of climax and completeness. Try a slight delay in starting the final stanza or a surge of extra energy or even a slight change in tempo. Near the end you might hold out a particular note or stretch out a phrase for extra expression.

## Through-composed songs

If the composer wrote new music for two or more parts of the poem, a song is said to be **through-composed,** even if it includes some pattern of repetition.

One common pattern is called **three-part song form,** in which there are two stanzas of music separated by a contrasting stanza.

## Pop-song form

Many popular and Broadway songs follow **pop-song form**. After an introductory **verse,** the **chorus** begins with an eight-measure melody, called the **first 8.** This is repeated with new words as the **second 8.** For contrast, a new eight-measure melody follows, called the **bridge** or **release.** Then the first melody comes back in the **return.**

"It Don't Mean a Thing" (page 220) is a good example of pop-song form:

- mm. 1–10    Introduction (ending with a **vamp**, which means that it can be repeated if the singer is not ready to begin)
- mm. 11–26   Verse (background reasons for the song)
- mm. 27–34   Chorus:        First 8
- mm. 35–42                   Second 8
- mm. 43–50                   Bridge
- mm. 51–58                   Return

Pop songs that are published as sheet music usually have repeat bars with a first and second ending so that the whole chorus can be sung or played a second time, if desired.

In one variation of pop-song form, the main sections of the song are each 16 measures long rather than 8. In another variation the chorus has an extra climactic ending in addition to the 32 (or 64) usual measures. In pop music an extra ending is called a **tag,** in classical music, a **coda.** Which other songs in this book have pop-song form? Which have tags?

Whether you are singing Broadway or classical songs, you can help your audience enjoy your song more if you make the form clear in your performance. Here are some ways:

- Allow some extra time, even a silence, between the verse and the chorus.
- Change your delivery in some way to call attention to the contrasting section or bridge; perhaps this is the time to move or change your posture.
- Slow down a little at the end of the bridge so that the return brings back the first tempo along with the melody.

These are suggestions; not every one will work in every song. Whatever song you sing, decide where its climax is. Often the climax is the highest note of the song; usually it is louder or softer than the rest of the song. Plan how you will build toward the climax and how you will relax the energy of the song afterward.

## The accompanist

Every thinking singer knows that the piano accompanist is a Very Important Person. A good accompanist can make you sing better than you ever thought you could. A poor one can make you sound as if you never practiced at all. A friendly accompanist makes it easy and pleasant for you to perform, but a thoughtless accompanist can drown you out and distract the audience from your performance. So find the best accompanist you can and treat that person well.

- *Give your accompanist good sheet music to play from.* I have seen someone walk into an audition, hand the pianist a folded, gray (illegal) photocopy, and say, "I sing this down a step from where it's written." Such behavior shows ignorance and poor planning. If the pianist cannot read the music or it falls off the music rack, the auditioner will blame you and nobody else.
- *Give your pianist enough time to learn the music.* Deliver your music to the pianist well ahead of the due date.
- *Respect your pianist's skill level.* Some pianists can **transpose** (play a song in a different key from the written one) and some cannot; very few are willing to transpose at sight. That is a complex skill that not every musician develops.
- *Take rehearsals seriously.* Prepare your music and arrive on time, ready to work. Rehearsals help each of you to understand how best to help the other.
- *Ask your pianist to express opinions* both about the music and about your singing. You can learn a lot from an experienced pianist. If you are singing

out of tune or have learned a wrong note, it is certainly wiser to let the pianist say so than to display the problem in public.

- *Let your accompanist feel well paid*, in money or in appreciation or both.

## Poise, confidence, and overcoming stage fright

By singing regularly for your voice teacher and other voice students you have gone a long way toward feeling comfortable about public performance.

Even so, it is natural to want to do your best in front of others. For some singers this natural desire to do well takes the exaggerated form of "stage fright" and gets in the way of their real goal of communication. Let's learn to minimize stage fright so that we enjoy the excitement of performing without the negative effects of fear.

Confidence lies in knowing that you can do well and that your listeners will like what you offer them. After all, you are gracious in recognizing the good in other singers' performances, and you should recognize the good in your own.

Some of us remember other persons in our past who judged us negatively (or we thought they did). It may be necessary to do some mental work to deal with those "internal judges." Here is one approach: Imagine your judges sitting in the audience while you perform, and picture smiles on their faces. (If those persons, in fact, cannot express any pleasant feelings, that is their problem.)

Should you not criticize yourself? Yes, in the practice room or in class, but *not at all onstage*.

Learn to criticize yourself objectively. Objective self-criticism sounds like this: "I forgot a word in the second verse, and I think I sang flat in the last phrase." Objective self-criticism says that you want to improve and gives others a chance to help you by agreeing or disagreeing with your evaluation of your performance.

Subjective self-criticism, or complaining, sounds like this: "I was awful, and I blew the whole thing!" Such criticism gets in the way of improvement and keeps you from thinking about specific ways to do better. Subjective self-criticism is tiresome to other people because it is self-centered. It shuts the door to comments from others. (If you say you sang terribly, then anyone who says otherwise must be ignorant or insincere or both.) Learn to thank others for their positive comments and to invite their suggestions for improvement.

## Preparation is the best confidence builder

The essential ingredient to confidence is preparation. As part of your daily practice, think of preparing for a performance: Can you sing well after eating? How much warm-up do you need? Can you sing your song acceptably every day, or only on rare occasions when you feel especially good?

As a performance approaches, learn what you can about the audience for whom you will sing. Visit the place and practice on the stage where you will perform, if possible. Practice with the instrument (or cassette or CD) that will be your accompaniment. Plan how you will enter and where you will stand. Plan what you will wear, and be sure that the neckline and waistline feel comfortable when you breathe.

Plan what you will say: Will you welcome the audience? Will you introduce yourself and your accompanist? Will you introduce your songs? Do you know how to pronounce the titles and composers of your songs? Being prepared is the key to confidence.

Here is the best advice I can give about performance nerves: If you can sing your songs well every day for a week before the performance, then you need have no fear about singing them on the performance day, too. The extra energy that comes from excitement will probably work in your favor.

But if a song is not reliable for you on a daily basis, then it is not yet time to sing it in public. Choose something more comfortable.

**Onstage**

After all of your preparations are done, performance onstage is a natural climax to a pleasant process. One of the best mental attitudes to maintain is that the stage is your home, that the members of the audience are your guests at a party, and that the music is entertainment (even the food) that you are offering to them. This little game of the imagination takes your attention away from yourself and focuses it on making sure that your listeners have a good time.

Performances of classical music are somewhat formal, but only because we want everyone to enjoy the music without any distraction or annoyance. Too much formality looks stiff and unfriendly; too much casualness looks careless and indifferent. Stage etiquette does not mean following a list of rules; it simply means doing things smoothly and without fuss.

The singer enters the stage first, followed by the accompanist and the page-turner, if any. Walk to your place at a normal rate. Avoid crossing in front of someone else, and avoid turning your back to the audience. If the audience welcomes you with applause, bow slightly to thank them. Simply lean forward enough to take a good look at your shoes; that is a bow.

If there is no printed program, you need to say hello to the audience and introduce yourself and your accompanist. Speak clearly, audibly, and slowly enough so that everyone can understand you. In addition to saying the name of your song and its composer, you may want to tell the audience something of interest about your song. People feel that they know you better if you speak as well as sing to them. You may find that their positive acceptance of what you say puts you more at ease.

It is impolite to confront your guests in a foreign language without offering to help them understand it. If your song is in a foreign language, the audience should have a translation in the printed program, or you should give them a brief summary. A good way to begin is: "In this song I am . . ."

When you are ready to sing, be sure that the first words of the song are in your mind. Take a good breath and let it out again silently, making sure that your breathing muscles are not stiff.

Agree beforehand on how the song will begin: Will you give a signal, or will the pianist decide when to begin? If the song has no piano introduction, ask the pianist to play a tonic chord quietly with your starting note as the top note of the chord. From the first note of the introduction, you are already in the mood of the song.

"Well begun is half done," says a wise proverb. Give full attention to the first notes you sing, making sure you give them enough time and enough energy to be heard clearly. Once the song is launched on its way, give your attention to the meaning of the words and what you want to say to the audience. Keep thinking ahead, so that when you end a phrase, the next phrase is already fully formed in your imagination.

"The eyes are the windows of the soul," says another proverb. Your listeners want more than just to hear your voice—they want you to communicate with them personally. In two or three minutes there is time to direct some of the song to every part of the audience. If you think that seeing faces may disturb you, try focusing on a point just between two persons' heads. Singing with your eyes either closed or raised to the ceiling is not a good practice; people quickly see that you are singing "over their heads," and their minds will tend to wander.

### "I don't know what to do with my hands."

First, relax them. If they are visibly tense, they act as magnets that draw the audience's attention away from what you are singing. Most of the time they belong at your sides. If they are uncomfortable there, you may rest one hand on the piano or hold both hands together at waist level (not below).

Keep the mood of the song through piano interludes, through all of your own singing (whether you are pleased with it or not), and through the postlude until the last note stops sounding.

May you use gestures? Yes, if they come easily. Pointless arm-waving detracts from the music, but so does unnatural stiffness. Let the music and words tell you what to do; a gesture that flows naturally from the meaning of the song will enhance your performance.

When the music ends and you let go of your concentration, the audience knows the song is over. Bow again modestly, just as you did before; a bow says, "Thank you for listening to me." After acknowledging the audience, smile at the accompanist, again to say, "Thank you." After a group of several songs or after a particularly difficult piece, gesture to your accompanist to stand and take a bow with you. Then you both leave the stage together, usually in the order in which you entered the stage.

## What about mishaps?

The best way to recover from a mistake is to stay in the mood of the song. Think ahead to the next phrase on which you and the pianist can get together and go on. Most mishaps go by without the audience knowing or caring; they still enjoy the song if you go on performing without giving off distress signals. If there are problems, it is not a good idea to flash a glance at the accompanist; the glance advertises the problem and looks like an attempt to put blame on the probably innocent pianist.

If something goes wrong, should you ever interrupt the song? Usually not, assuming that you can save the mood and the message of the song. But sometimes a song really needs to start over. For instance, if your pianist completely stops playing—perhaps the music fell or you got started on the wrong note—everyone knows that something is wrong and needs to be fixed.

Keep looking ahead to the goal: communicating a message to the audience.

## If you are ill

Courtesy in performance means that the audience's pleasure and comfort comes ahead of your own. If you do not feel well, you decide (with your teacher) whether to sing or not. Do not worry the audience by making an apology about being sick. An apology makes people fear that you may be hurting your voice on their account.

And, well or ill, be courteous and positive after a performance, even if you are disappointed with your own singing. Anyone who has enjoyed your singing deserves to receive your thanks, not your disappointment over slight mishaps.

## About committees

A special note to college students and to singers who enter competitions or sing before a committee or "jury" of voice teachers. Rather than being a tough, super-critical audience, voice teachers are the most sympathetic listeners you could have. They have heard many beginners, and they know the pitfalls of singing. Voice teachers are intensely interested in voices, otherwise they would not be in their profession, and they sincerely want you to succeed. Sing to them as you would to an audience of friends. Forgive them if the wearisome duty of writing criticisms and giving grades sometimes causes them to behave in a way that is not their best.

And if you are lucky enough to get a criticism, take it as a suggestion for improvement and something you can use to do better next time.

*Additional reading*   *If you only read one book about acting and show business, read:*

*Audition: Everything an Actor Needs to Know to Get the Part* by Michael Shurtleff. Bantam Books, 1978.

*For insight into style and interpretation in classical music, read the song analyses in:*

*The Art of Accompanying* by Robert Spillman. Schirmer Books, 1985.

*More important than any reading: your own attendance at events when others perform. Observe, think, and learn.*

ALWAYS Remember that *you* are the host at the party.

ALWAYS Remember that your audience *wants* to hear what you want to sing for them.

# 10 Extending Your Voice

*Guiding Questions:* ***How can I go on building my voice to make it stronger?***
***How can I develop my breath for better control over phrasing and dynamics?***
***How can I learn to sing quick patterns, like scales and ornaments?***
***How can I sing better low notes and better high notes?***

Your vocal exercises until now have focused on the middle range, where most singing is done. When you and your teacher agree that this central core of your voice feels and sounds right, you are ready to extend your voice.

As you work on your voice, use a balance of ambition and patience. Keep an open attitude when your teacher asks you to try something new. Reach a little beyond what you can do now, so that your voice will grow.

But vocal growth cannot be forced by overworking the voice. If you ever hear hoarseness or feel pain, stop and rest a few minutes and change the exercise.

## Vocal strength

The vocal folds are not the kind of muscle that becomes bulkier with exercise. The voice gains in power and stamina by becoming more efficient, more effective in resonating the sound that comes from the tiny vocal folds. Breath management is the aspect of singing that benefits most from improvements in your general fitness.

A physician who examines your vocal folds will see little, if any, change in them as a result of vocal study. But their actions change according to your mental concepts. As you imagine a desired tone quality, the vocal folds and resonators adjust to produce the imagined sound as nearly as they can. Repeated practice brings finer tuning, producing the results you want more perfectly and easily.

Because your imagination guides the whole process of vocal growth, you must be aware and alert during practice. If you try to strengthen your voice by singing scales without concentrating on them, you will only train bad habits and hurt your voice.

In chapter 3 we said, "Let your feelings be the key to vocal resonance." Your will to communicate with others is still the best motivation to increase your vocal resonance.

## Focus

**Mental focus** aims to direct the voice toward a goal. When you throw a ball at a target, you think about the target and not about your arm. Just as your brain tells your arm how to throw, it will tell your vocal muscles how to make a tone reach listeners at the back of an auditorium. Your breath does not blow the voice across the room; rather, your voice creates sound waves that travel across a distance.

Mental focus works in other ways, also. Some singers improve their vocal cord function by **visualizing** the smooth, complete contact of the vocal folds as if watching them on a screen.

Many singers also use mental focus in the form called **voice placement.** Most good singers feel concentrated vibrations that accompany their best tones. By recalling the vibrating sensations, singers learn to reproduce the good singing that caused them.

Steady breath supply is a prerequisite for focused tone, and often a weak tone can be reinforced by improving the breath supply. Singing on sustained, buzzing consonants is an excellent way to assure that the breath supply is steady and energetic. Especially good are the voiced consonants [z], [ʒ] and [ð], which direct air through a narrow channel toward the front teeth.

**Increasing resonance**

A technique that often helps to increase resonance is this: with your thumbs resting on each side of your jaw, let the tips of your longest fingers meet in front of the bridge of your nose. This forms a little "porch" in front of your face; keep your elbows down and arms relaxed so that the porch is not too wide. When you sing into the "porch," you will feel more willing to let the tone go free. Then take your hands away and try to feel the same sensations of vocal freedom.

**Figure 10.1**

## Improving breath control

Breath control improves when vocal tone becomes more concentrated. Good tone is efficient: it has maximum resonance with a minimum expenditure of air.

After a few initial lessons you may find that good breath support occurs automatically when tonal concepts are correct. But if your breathing is not working automatically, review the lessons learned in chapter 3:

- Do your lower ribs expand, including the lower back?
- Do the abdominal muscles relax outward freely to let breath flow in?
- Do the lower ribs remain expanded when you begin to sing?
- Do you support the singing tone with energized abdominal muscles?

Centuries ago singers discovered a test for efficient tone production: Hold a lighted candle a few inches in front of your open mouth while you sing a vowel. If the candle flickers, too much air is escaping. Try it. When you can vocalize

**Figure 10.2**

**Figure 10.3**

*If you sing lying down, gravity (A) draws your abdomen toward the floor. Your diaphragm, pushing in the direction of arrow B, resists the fall of the abdominal organs and prevents them from pushing the air out of your body too fast.*

without making the candle flame waver, you will understand that good singing takes much less air than one would think.

"Drink the tone in" is an example of a mental concept that singers use to economize their breath. Even though air is leaving the body, the thought of air coming into the body slows the rate of movement.

As the abdominal muscles move inward, supporting the breath, the diaphragm resists them, slowing down their motion. You can sense this by singing while lying down on the floor. Use a book to pillow your head, and sing as normally as possible.

Another trick singers use is to wear an elastic belt that pulls in the abdomen. Instead of pulling the abdomen in more quickly, the belt energizes the muscles to resist collapse. Sporting goods stores sell an elastic "tummy trimmer" to be worn while exercising. It is about seven inches wide and is fastened with Velcro so that it fits anyone.

A

B

## Agility

Most styles of music require **agility,** also called flexibility, the ability to sing notes rapidly. Agility includes the scales, trills and vocal ornaments used by classical singers and the quick flourishes of notes called "licks" that are sung by blues and jazz singers. Learning agility in any style requires training the ear to hear quickly as well as the voice to move quickly.

In some musical styles a singer sings only the written notes, but other styles allow freedom to improvise and add ornaments at will.

Certain standardized ornaments have been compared to the compulsory figures practiced by ice skaters. As in every other aspect of singing, the main ingredient is your musical imagination. If you can form a quick ornament clearly in your mind, your brain will tell your voice how to sing it.

## Exercise

**10.1 Upper Neighbors.** The most basic ornament is alternation between a melody note and the neighbor note above it. This exercise uses an upper neighbor (UN) and some common variations based on it. Try these patterns, which can be used in various styles of music. Purpose: to make the voice flexible.

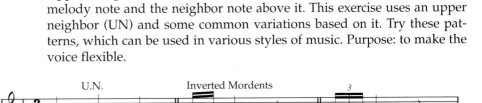

CD 1 Track 33

## Range

I have never yet met a student who had a small vocal range, but I have known many who limited themselves to a small range. They felt unsure of new sensations and unfamiliar tones. They needed confidence and guidance to learn to accept their full vocal range.

Your voice almost certainly has a range of two octaves or more (unless there is a problem that deserves therapy, such as nodules). Your full range may extend beyond three octaves if you include the lowest tones, even the soft breathy ones below the normal chest tones, and the lightest high tones, falsetto in men and "whistle tones" in women, which seem useless for singing but play an important role in extending range.

How much of your range can you use for singing songs? The answer depends on:

- The amount of freedom your vocal mechanism has when it adjusts to register changes;
- The musical styles you prefer to sing and whether they use a wide range; and
- Your personal willingness to accept the sounds that are natural to various registers of your voice.

**Low notes**

If you speak at a pitch near the lower end of your vocal range, your low notes probably already feel strong. If this is the case, you may find that vocal study changes your lower voice much less than it changes your upper voice. (If your low notes seem to become weaker as you develop the highs, this is an illusion. The low voice simply has less growing to do.)

To reach the maximum power of your low notes, you may need no more than a few reminders to focus and use your tonal energy. (Even a natural bass may feel shy about using the strong low notes that are his special gift.) Often, however, young women hesitate to use chest tones, feeling that they are ugly or unmusical.

One way to discover how much energy the chest voice needs is to speak the words of a song vigorously and then to concentrate on the same physical sensations while singing the same words.

Another way to learn about the chest voice is to use a deliberately ugly, "brassy" sound in the syllable "quack."

**Exercises**

**10.2 Quack-quack.** Use lots of energy. There is no way to make this beautiful, so have fun with it. Move your jaw, lips, and tongue freely, without tension. Sing the pattern in various keys in the lower part of your range. Practice this for only a few minutes at a time.

When you vocalize to strengthen the resonance of low notes, it is important to use a bright tone quality and good posture. Lowering your head does not help; it merely restricts the freedom of the throat.

CD 1 Track 34

**10.3 Low Scale and Turn.** Look straight ahead and keep your posture. Sing very legato and drop the jaw low. After the 4-note scale, observe the rest, but do not take a breath; sing the **turn** on the same breath. Purpose: to focus resonance for the lowest tones.

CD 1 Track 35

**High notes**

High notes develop more noticeably than low notes for many students simply because the high voice has not been used much and it responds quickly to encouragement.

If high tones come easily to you, accept the gift with thanks and use it with pleasure. Most people need time and practice to develop high tones because of the fine adjustment needed between breath energy and vocal fold function.

One biological function of the vocal folds is to close tightly when the breath is put under pressure, as in lifting a heavy weight. When the vocal folds sense high air pressure, a reflex closes them tightly to hold it back. A singer has to overcome this natural reflex so that the vocal folds gently close the right amount for singing; they must not clutch and stop the airflow entirely.

Upper tones can be found gently with exercises 1.6 and 1.7. Start without a pitch from the piano. Sing a high pitch first, then find out what it was. You are singing spontaneously, instead of trying to force the voice to sing tones that it may not be ready for. Now vocalize downward a few times. When you repeat this process, you may find that the voice has warmed up and is ready for a somewhat higher note. You can also do this with any of the hum consonants or with the "Bubble" used in exercise 2.6.

If you start an exercise in a low key and move it up gradually, go only as high as you can sing with a feeling of freedom and ease in your throat. If your throat tightens, rest for at least a few seconds and then start over with a different exercise.

Consider this quotation from a voice teacher of long experience, Oren Brown, formerly of the Juilliard School in New York City: "Take only what the voice gives you." And here is another that he has said often: "Think the tone and let it happen."

An easy way to discover and practice high notes is the "Open-mouth Hum," described by another prominent voice teacher, the late Dr. Berton Coffin. It resembles an [m] hum, but the jaw can be more open because the lips are not closed.

## Exercises

**10.4  Open-mouth Hum.** Sing [a], but cover your mouth completely either with the palm of your hand or with the back of your hand. No air escapes from your mouth; the air and the tone pass through your nose instead. Repeat the phrase with your mouth open. Purpose: to discover a light, free approach to higher notes.

CD 1 Track 36

Singing "behind the hand" can be used to practice any vowel and any musical phrase. It helps many women to discover "whistle" tones on "High C" and above. These tones are very small at first, but they may develop to usable strength.

**10.5  Two-octave Scale.** Sing softly on [i] or any vowel that is easy for you. If the voice breaks or skips notes at the register changes, start again more softly. Find at least one starting tone on which you can do this long scale easily. Purpose: to learn to pass through register changes smoothly.

CD 1 Track 37

**10.6 Three Scales—3 + 5 + 9.** Sing the three scales separately at first. Later combine them into one long phrase. Practice at various volume levels, not always loud or always soft. Purpose: to exercise the voice quickly and lightly through a wider range, while building flexibility.

CD 1 Track 38

**10.7 Legato Chords.** Sing very smoothly. Feel a special continuity between the contrasting vowels [i] and [ɔ]. Close [ɔ] to [o] on any note that seems easier that way. Purpose: to exercise higher tones on dark vowels.

CD 1 Track 39

*Additional reading*

*For a host of ideas about the next steps in your vocal development:*

*Discover Your Voice: How to Develop Healthy Voice Habits* by Oren Brown. Singular Publishing Group, 1996.

*Dozens of exercises for range extension are given in:*

*Coffin's Overtones of Bel Canto* by Berton Coffin. Scarecrow Press, 1980.

---

ALWAYS Release the tongue forward.
  (Never tighten or pull back on it.)

ALWAYS Let the larynx maintain a resting position.
  (Not pressed down or lifted up.)

ALWAYS Be mindful of what your body is telling you.
  (Discomfort means that some of your work is being wasted.)

# 11 | Understanding Your Vocal Instrument

*Guiding Questions:* ***Physically, how does the voice work?***
***How can I keep it healthy?***

## The voice as a musical instrument

All musical instruments have three essential elements:

- A **motor,** which provides and transmits energy;
- A **vibrator,** which converts the energy into audible vibrations (musical pitches); and
- A **resonator,** which strengthens the tones and modifies them by selectively strengthening certain overtones.

In the case of a trumpet, for instance, the motor is the player's breath, the vibrator is the player's lips, while the brass tubing forms the resonator. Can you identify the three basic elements of a violin? a clarinet? a bass drum? a piano?

The human voice has a fourth element, an articulator, which forms speech sounds. No other instrument can produce words. A voice can produce a wide variety of tone colors, and with articulation adding exact meaning and poetic appeal, the voice has tremendous potential to communicate emotions.

All four elements of the voice must coordinate perfectly to produce the freest, most expressive singing. They are:

1. **Motor,** or actuator: breath pressure, coming from the lungs.
2. **Vibrators:** vocal folds (commonly called the vocal cords), located in the larynx. Breath flow sets them in motion, and they produce a buzzing sound that is our basic vocal tone.
3. **Resonators:** the entire passageway from the vocal folds up to the lips and nose. The resonators we can control are in the throat and mouth. Others are in the nasal passages and, perhaps, the sinuses. Acoustical science has not yet answered all of our questions about resonance.
4. **Articulators:** the flexible tongue and lips acting against the inflexible teeth and hard palate, influenced also by the angle of the jaw.

## What's behind your Adam's apple?

When all goes well, we sing without knowing or thinking anything about our throats. But when we are sick or feel other vocal problems, then it helps to know the most important parts of the vocal instrument and how they work. The description given here uses some medical terms that are useful to know when you are communicating with your physician. The numbers refer to figure 11.1, which uses common English terms instead of the medical ones.

**Figure 11.1**

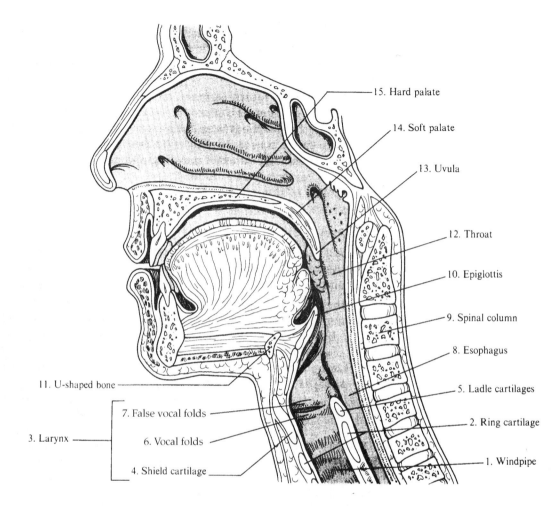

15. Hard palate

14. Soft palate

13. Uvula

12. Throat

10. Epiglottis

9. Spinal column

8. Esophagus

5. Ladle cartilages

2. Ring cartilage

1. Windpipe

11. U-shaped bone

3. Larynx

7. False vocal folds

6. Vocal folds

4. Shield cartilage

Air from the lungs rises through the right and left bronchial tubes, which join to form the **trachea** (#1, windpipe). Just above your breastbone you can feel the bumpy partial rings of cartilage that hold the windpipe open. The only complete ring is the top one, the **cricoid cartilage** (#2, ring cartilage). It is larger than the rest and forms the base of the **larynx** (#3, voice box). (Larynx rhymes with "rare inks"; the plural is larynges [lærɪndʒiz]).

A large larynx shows as a bump, but a smaller one may be harder to locate. The part of the larynx that can be felt under the skin is the **thyroid cartilage** (#4, shield cartilage). It is formed of two flat surfaces that meet in front at an angle. The angle is wider in women, making the larynx flatter, and narrower in men, forming the Adam's apple.

The thyroid cartilage, which is soft in children but turns to bone during the early twenties, protects the windpipe from closing. Without it, even a light pressure on the neck could cut off our air supply. (The **thyroid gland** has a similar shape; it is located in front of the windpipe, a little below the thyroid cartilage.)

The vocal folds, described below, attach at their forward ends inside the point where the sides of the thyroid cartilage meet. The vocal folds stretch over the top of the open windpipe and attach at the rear end to two tiny cartilages, the right and left **arytenoid cartilages** (#5, ladle cartilages, located there but hidden in the tissue). The ladles slide along the upper surface of the ring cartilage. By means of a complex musculature they can move together and apart and tip forward, back and to the side, always moving counter to each other. The vocal folds are always close to each other at the front ends, but the arytenoids pull them apart at the rear when we breathe in and bring them together again when we speak or sing.

The ring, the shield, and the two ladles form the stiff framework of the larynx. Cartilages are flexible in children, harden as we mature, and eventually turn to bone. This is one of the reasons why voice quality changes with age. The inner surfaces of the larynx are covered with **mucous membrane.** When it is irritated by infection, you have "laryngitis," and you may lose your voice.

What really interests us are the **vocal folds** (#6). Voice scientists now reject the common term "vocal cords," because they are not like strings at all; rather, each one is like a shelf on the inside surface of the larynx covered by a fold of cloth. The main part of each vocal fold is a thyro-arytenoid muscle, named for the two cartilages where the ends of the muscle are attached. The edges of the folds, where the finest adjustments for singing take place, are formed of a white membrane that also covers their under-surfaces. When the folds are apart, the space between them is called the **glottis,** shown in figure 11.2.

Just above the vocal folds are two similar folds, called the **false vocal folds** (#7). They play no direct role in voice production, but they sometimes come together to help close the wind passage, for instance, when lifting a heavy weight. The space between the true and the false folds may be a significant resonator.

Directly behind the larynx is the top of the **esophagus** (#8, foodpipe), which is closed flat against the **spinal column** (#9) except when something passes through it on the way to the stomach. Food and drink going to the esophagus have to cross over the larynx without falling into it. The top of the larynx is guarded by a leaf-shaped cartilage, the **epiglottis** (#10). Attached to the upper front edge of the shield cartilage, the epiglottis stands nearly upright most of the time, but during swallowing it falls down and back and covers the larynx. If it does not work properly, we choke.

The **hyoid bone** (#11, U-shaped bone) is located above the larynx at the base of the tongue; you may be able to feel the ends of it on either side of your neck just below the jaw. It forms part of the flexible suspension system from which the larynx hangs. A way to sense this system is to place the backs of your fingers on either side of the larynx and move it from side to side.

The open space that forms the main resonator for singing is the **pharynx** (#12, throat). When you yawn in front of the mirror, you can see the moist back wall of the pharynx. An infection there causes an inflammation called pharyngitis, which is often painful but does not always affect your voice. The open space extends upward to the naso-pharynx, which connects to the nasal passages.

When you are looking in the mirror to find your pharynx, you can't help noticing your **uvula** (Latin for "little grape," #13), which hangs down from the **velum** (#14, soft palate). The soft palate can drop down and hide your pharynx, or it can rise up to expose quite a bit of the pharyngeal wall.

The soft palate determines how much of your breath passes through your nose and how much through your mouth. If your soft palate is too low, too much breath passes through the nose and your tone sounds nasal. If your soft palate is too high, it can seal off the nasal passage so that you cannot say [m] or [n], and you sound like a person stopped up with a cold. Most voice teachers recommend keeping the palate high but not closing off the nasal passages.

In front of the soft palate is the bony **hard palate** (#15). By running your tongue back along the roof of your mouth you can feel where the hard palate ends.

Above the palate are the nasal passages, left and right. They are separated by a bony partition (septum). The sides of the nasal passages are lined with irregular projections that serve, like the surface of a radiator, to warm the air as it goes by.

Other parts of the vocal mechanism—the tongue, lips, jaw, and teeth—are all familiar and visible.

## Vocal health

To better understand vocal health, let's look more closely at the vocal folds themselves. Figure 11.2 shows how they appear to a laryngologist looking down a person's throat with a dental mirror. The vocal folds are seen while closing to make a sound, but not yet fully closed.

**Figure 11.2**

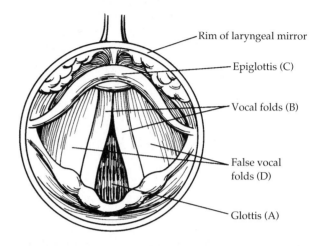

Rim of laryngeal mirror

Epiglottis (C)

Vocal folds (B)

False vocal folds (D)

Glottis (A)

At the center of the picture is a shaded space, the glottis (A), which opens into the windpipe. With a light the doctor can see the rings of the windpipe from inside.

On either side of the glottis are the vocal folds (B). In this mirror image the point where the vocal folds meet at the front of the larynx is toward the top of the picture but out of sight, hidden underneath the erect epiglottis (C). The rear end of the vocal folds is toward the bottom of the picture, also out of sight. The vocal folds look white and smooth when they are rested and healthy, pinkish after vigorous use. Only the central part of the vocal folds can be seen because on each side they are hidden by the pink upper surfaces of the false vocal folds (D).

Here are some essential facts about the vocal folds:

1. They are tiny. A soprano's vocal folds are stretched over a round opening with about the same diameter as a dime. The vocal folds of a bass are stretched over an opening the size of a nickel. These small muscles do remarkable feats for us.

2. On most tones in your range, the vocal folds touch each other and separate again once for each vibration. On middle C, which is in everyone's range, your vocal folds touch each other 262 times per second. They also part 262 times per second and let 262 puffs of air escape, causing a wave movement in the air. A listener hears this wave as a tone with the pitch called middle C and a frequency of 262 Hz (Herz, or cycles per second).

| 65.5 Hz | 131 Hz | 262 Hz | = | 262 Hz | 524 Hz | 1,048 Hz |

*"Middle C"*                    *"High C"*

When a man sings the C below middle C, his folds touch each other only 131 times per second (Hz), but if a woman sings the C above middle C, there are 524 such events. A soprano's high C has 1048 Hz, but at that speed the folds probably do not close entirely. Can you imagine how many thousands of times the folds open and close in a song? Clearly, if there is anything rough, inefficient or unnecessarily forceful about the singing tone, the contact edges of the vocal folds will be subjected to considerable friction, even chafing.

3. Like the diaphragm, the vocal folds have no proprioceptive nerves, no way of telling us if they are being hurt. This assures that the vocal folds always function and never shy away from pain. Throat pain comes from over-worked muscles or infected tissues nearby.

4. When our vocal folds are abused or infected, the body tries to heal them by sending extra liquids to the scene: extra mucus to cover their surfaces and extra blood to heal internal damage. Increased blood supply turns the vocal folds pink or red, and they swell up.

5. When the folds swell slightly, the first sign of trouble may be hoarseness, meaning that the edges are not closing perfectly and air is escaping between them. They may be unable to form the thin edges needed for high tones. If we go on trying to talk and sing, pain may develop as nearby muscles strain to take over the work of the vocal folds. If the vocal folds swell too much, their edges become bumpy, perhaps unable to meet and form tones at all. Then we lose our voices and have to rest them until the swelling goes down. The blood vessels in swollen folds are vulnerable to injury because their walls are stretched thin.

## Vocal overuse

The facts you have just read about the vocal folds explain why *overuse causes more voice problems than any other factor*. Enthusiastic, energetic singers love to socialize and enjoy expressing their emotions. It's not surprising that many of us overuse our voices.

Vocal overuse, medically called "hyperfunction," includes:

- Shouting, for instance, cheering at a sports event;
- Loud talking and laughing, for instance, at a noisy party;
- Insistent talking, as when we try to dominate others;
- Talking or singing over the noise of a moving car or other machinery;
- Coughing and throat clearing, which violently rub the folds against each other;
- Singing at an inappropriate pitch level, as when one is placed in the wrong section of a choir;
- Singing longer and louder than we can do with comfort, whether that means singing with a rock group or getting carried away at an exciting choral rehearsal.

The limits of safe vocal use differ a great deal from one individual to another. Most of us learn our limits by the unhappy experience of hoarseness or temporary voice loss. I love to cheer at a football game, but if it takes three or four days for the vocal folds to repair themselves, was the fun worth it?

## Damaged voices

Fortunately our vocal folds are resilient. If we stop the overuse and allow the folds to rest, they usually heal themselves. If overuse continues and the folds do not have time to rest, a persistent bump called a vocal node or nodule may develop on the edge of one or both folds. Nodes prevent the folds from closing correctly and cause reduction of range and volume. *Only a physician can correctly diagnose vocal nodes.*

In case of persistent hoarseness, consult a physician to find out whether you have nodes. In the early stages they are soft and often heal with a few weeks of rest and reduced voice use. In later stages they grow progressively harder and require more rest to heal.

Nodes are probably not the fault of your voice teacher, who sees you for only a short time each week and cannot possibly monitor all your activities.

If nodes require treatment, your first step should be to consult a speech therapist who can help you identify vocally abusive habits in your daily life and replace them with safer ones. Nodes rarely require surgical removal. (Never undertake surgery without a second or third medical opinion.)

**Defense against colds**

If you have been exposed to a virus, your first line of respiratory defense is: *Keep your vocal tract moist.*

Your entire vocal tract is lined with mucous membrane, which produces moisture. We may notice mucus only when sickness makes it thick and annoying, but a constant, unnoticed flow of mucus is essential to our health and comfort. Microorganisms and foreign particles that land on mucous membrane stick to the wet surface and are carried away on the cleansing stream of moisture. If the membrane is dry, the particles irritate the body tissue and microorganisms can launch their attack.

## Colds and flu

Common colds are caused by any of 200 viruses. There is no cure, not even antibiotics. Try to avoid colds, but if one develops anyway, treat the symptoms until they clear up in a week or two.

Steps to preventing and avoiding colds and influenzas:

Keep your resistance up with a good diet and enough rest

Drink plenty of liquids and humidify your environment if possible

Wash your hands often, especially if you are around people with colds

Keep your hands away from your nose, mouth, and eyes

Avoid letting your body become chilled, because viruses thrive at a temperature somewhat lower than our normal body temperature. After long exposure to cold, a warm bath or shower may help raise your resistance.

To treat a cold or flu that has begun, increase all of the above and also:

Take acetaminophen to reduce fever and relieve aches. *Never use aspirin* or products that contain it because they dilate the capillaries that supply blood to the vocal folds. The thin walls of the swollen capillaries can rupture and hemorrhage.

Avoid antihistamines; they dry out the throat as well as the nose

If you need a nasal decongestant spray for a stuffy nose, use it for no more than three days.

A cold or flu may be accompanied by a bacterial infection that is treatable with antibiotics, for instance, strep throat. If any of these symptoms show up, see a physician promptly: severe difficulty in swallowing; fever of 101°F or higher; fever that lasts four days or more; a cough that produces rusty or green mucus.

As for singing and voice lessons when you are not well, ask your teacher's advice. If vocal rest is in order, that means

Talking quietly and less than usual

No singing, shouting, or laughing

No whistling or loud whispering, both of which use the vocal folds.

For any vocal disorder that lasts more than three or four days, see a physician who will examine your vocal folds. Before your office visit, restudy the vocal anatomy described in this chapter. As an informed patient, you can ask better questions and help the doctor to help you.

Heated and air-conditioned buildings, as well as automobiles and airplanes, usually have air that is unnaturally dry. Using an ultrasonic vaporizer, especially in your sleeping room, may help you avoid respiratory infections. Drinking lots of liquids also helps, especially water at medium temperature. Avoid diuretics, like caffeine, which drain moisture from our tissues.

While keeping your humidity high, you can also keep your immunity as high as possible with reasonable rest, avoidance of stress, good nourishment that includes vitamin C, and, yes, a good mental attitude.

Tobacco smoke obviously dries out our throat tissues. Marijuana smoke is even hotter because it is unfiltered. Don't smoke either one. Cocaine and crack lead to even worse respiratory problems.

## Hearing

Living from day to day in the modern world involves a problem that must be taken up here: noise and noise damage. Many young singers and musicians are finding by the age of 30 that their hearing has already been damaged permanently by the high sound levels of amplified music.

The ear drum, which receives sound vibrations that are carried in the air, is quite strong. But in the inner ear the sound vibrations are carried in a fluid medium, which moves microscopic hairlike cells. In a manner that is not completely understood, the hair cells convert the vibrations into nerve impulses that the brain interprets as sound. Unfortunately, loud noise damages the hair cells so that they lie down like so much trampled grass. But they do not stand up again, and there is no way to repair them. There are millions of them, but loud noises can also disable them in large numbers. The resulting loss of hearing is permanent.

Some studies show that old people do not naturally lose their hearing; rather, deafness is a result of the noise of civilized life. It is wrong to think "I'll be deaf someday anyway." You can safeguard your hearing. It is a vital line of communication, the sense that lets you enjoy music!

Steps to take:

- Listen to music at moderate sound levels, especially when using headphones;
- Avoid noisy environments, where you have to shout to be heard;
- Cover your ears if you expect loud noise, for instance, a fire engine approaching;
- Carry earplugs with you and use them, for instance, in movie theaters.

You are not alone in caring for your hearing. Many rock musicians wear inconspicuous earplugs on stage. Even some musicians in symphony orchestras protect their hearing with earplugs or with transparent partitions that shield them from the loud percussion instruments behind them.

## Additional reading

*The grandfather of voice books, now revised and in its second quarter century:*

*Keep Your Voice Healthy* by Friedrich Brodnitz, M.D., 2nd ed., College-Hill Press, 1987.

*The Journal of Singing,* published by the National Association of Teachers of Singing, contains invaluable articles on vocal health and the latest research in vocal science. This journal can be found in your local public or college library.

ALWAYS Drink plenty of water daily.
(Products that contain caffeine or alcohol do not count because they remove water from the body.)

ALWAYS Avoid smoking and secondhand smoke.
(Tobacco and other forms of smoke dry out and irritate the vocal mechanism.)

ALWAYS Protect your hearing.
(Avoid noisy environments and use earplugs when needed.)

# 12 | A Vocabulary for Music

**Guiding Questions:**

*Do I have a "musical ear"?*

*How do musicians think about rhythm? What is a measure? What is syncopation?*

*What does "in a key" mean? What is a scale?*

*What can I learn from looking at a piece of printed music?*

THIS chapter is for you to read anytime on your own or whenever your teacher assigns it. Even if you play an instrument and already know how to read notes, you may find some useful tips here.

When a new acquaintance learns that I teach singing, that person often responds with excuses about a lack of musical background. Here are some things people say and answers I might give if the other person is willing to listen:

*"Oh, I don't know a thing about music!"* Yes, you do. You are familiar with a tremendous amount of music. You just need a vocabulary to talk about it.

*"I hated piano lessons when I was a kid, but now I wish I'd kept on with them."* Don't feel guilty about your childhood music lessons. If you're willing to spend the time, you can still learn.

*"I love to sing, but my family all say I have a tin ear."* Sing anyway! Enjoy! When you find the right group of people to sing with, you will fit right in.

You do not need to apologize because other people had music lessons or home experiences that you did not have. Whatever you learn, starting now, will enrich your life through increased awareness of the music all around you.

## What is a musical ear?

Musicians do not all have a mysterious faculty that others lack. Everyone has a "musical ear" to some degree. Like other mental skills, the ability to remember and reproduce musical pitches varies a great deal from person to person, and it improves with training.

A few persons have so-called **perfect pitch,** the ability to name a pitch that is heard or sing any note at will. Most professional musicians have some degree of **relative pitch,** the ability to recognize or to sing particular notes with some reliability. Neither perfect nor relative pitch is essential for you to learn to sing melodies easily and correctly.

Are you **tone-deaf?** It's not very likely. Even if someone gave you that label, you probably can easily hear the difference between two melodies and even hear wrong or out-of-tune notes in a melody. Most people who think they are tone-deaf simply have not developed the ear-to-brain-to-throat coordination necessary for singing in tune.

Sometimes a "pitch problem" disappears when the singer realizes what vocal register to use. Other cases improve with proper guidance, time, and experience in a supportive group-singing environment.

## Rhythm

Rhythm is the life pulse of music, so important that there are exciting pieces of music that are played by drums alone without a single melody.

Rhythm is defined as organization in time. This may be nonmusical—"rhythm of breathing"—or musical—"march rhythm."

Musical rhythm involves repeated patterns of longer and shorter tones or stronger and weaker accents or both. Babies notice repeated movements and sounds and respond to them with pleasure. The most primitive rhythm is simple repetition of a steady beat:

/ / / / / / / / / / / / / / / / / / / / /

A baby notices such regularity and enjoys it, but does not respond the same way if strong beats are put in randomly, like this:

| / / | | / / / | / | / / | / / / | / / | /

Pleasurable musical rhythm begins when the stronger beats occur in a pattern, like this four-beat pattern:

| / / / | / / / | / / / | / / / | / / / |

or this three-beat pattern:

| / / | / / | / / | / / | / / | / / |

Most of our music is organized in patterns of two, three, or four beats. You can try these out in a simple exercise. Tap a steady beat with your left hand on a table or on your knees, and tap stronger beats with your right hand: every second, then every third, then every fourth, like this:

```
R    R    R    R    R    R    R
|    |    |    |    |    |    |
L L  L L  L L  L L  L L  L L  L L
```

```
R         R         R         R         R
|         |         |         |         |
L L L  L L L  L L L  L L L  L L L  L
```

```
R              R              R              R
|              |              |              |
L L L L  L L L L  L L L L  L L L L
```

## Measures and bar lines

In written music, the beginning of a beat pattern is shown by a vertical line called a **measure bar** or **bar line.** The music between two bar lines is one **measure** or **bar** of music.

The note just to the right of the bar line is always a strong beat. It is called a **downbeat,** because of the downward movement of a conductor's arm to start a measure. Often a phrase of music begins with an **upbeat,** which consists of one or two or more notes that prepare for the downbeat. Think of the melody to "He's

Got the Whole World in His Hands." What word comes on the first downbeat? How many upbeat notes come before that downbeat? What word comes on the second downbeat? (Check your answers by looking at the music on page 97.)

The diagrams of 4- and 3-beat patterns imply that downbeats are naturally louder than the beats in between, but that is not always so. When gospel or jazz singers clap, they clap after the downbeat, not with it. This creates strong accents that are perceived as offbeat, rather than on the downbeat:

```
   R    R     R     R     R     R     R
   |    |     |     |     |     |     |
L  L  L  L  L  L  L  L  L  L  L  L  L  L
```

Downbeats are established by means other than loudness, such as:

- Patterns of notes in the accompaniment that repeat in every measure;
- Chord changes on the first beat of each measure;
- Word accents.

**Rhythmic values**

In addition to notes that equal one beat, there are notes that last less or more than a beat. Visually all have oval heads. The longest note, called a **whole note** (usually lasting for four beats), is simply an empty oval. Adding a vertical stem makes a **half note** (two beats), filling it in makes a **quarter note** (one beat), and each added flag cuts the length of the note in half again.

Ways to produce other note lengths include:

- Combining consecutive notes on the same line or space with a curved line, a **tie**;
- Adding one-half to the length of a note with a **dot**;
- **Bracketing** three notes together with an indication that they take up the time value of two, or two notes together in a context of three-note groups.

On pages 91–92 are melodies that are graded to let you practice reading notes. You can use them right now to practice reading rhythms without singing.

Here's how: Use one or both hands to tap the basic beat on the edge of a desk, table or music stand. Place each beat in a separate place, like this: the downbeat directly in front of your body, each subsequent beat to the right (or to the left with your left hand). Return your hand to the starting place for each downbeat. The larger movement used in returning to the downbeat is a reminder that the downbeat is stronger than the others.

While your hand keeps the beat going steadily, say "Tah" out loud for every note. Use a lively voice and make each "Tah" last the right length of time for each note.

**Syncopation**

There can be a sense of surprise or fun when an event in the music suddenly goes against a set pattern. Perhaps a strong high note comes on a beat that is normally weak and then holds over to the next strong beat. Perhaps an emphatic word occurs in a weak part of the measure; or perhaps when we expect a downbeat there is a rest instead, and the expected note comes a half-beat late.

Such ways of shifting the measure accent are called **syncopation.** In a song a syncopation can result from a word of text coming a little sooner or a bit later than we expect it.

Study and practice the syncopations that appear in melodies on page 92, beginning with no. 15.

> "...when you have any friend to sing with you, you may practice together, which will sooner make you perfect than if you should study never so much by yourself."
> Thomas Morley, *A Plain & Easy Introduction to Practical Music,* 1597

## Pitches

When Maria in *The Sound of Music* starts to teach music to the von Trapp children, she makes up a song, "Do-Re-Mi," page 96. The seven syllables **Do, Re, Mi, Fa, So, La,** and **Ti** are widely used names for the notes of the scale. Because we hear tones as being "lower" and "higher," it makes sense to arrange the names of the tones vertically, from the bottom up, like this:

| | | |
|---|---|---|
| 8 | C | Do |
| 7 | B | Ti |
| 6 | A | La |
| 5 | G | So |
| 4 | F | Fa |
| 3 | E | Mi |
| 2 | D | Re |
| 1 | C | Do |

Sing up a scale, starting from the lowest note and singing "One, two, three..." (It doesn't matter just now whether the starting note is really C.) Sing back down the scale: "Eight, seven, six..." (It sounds like the Christmas song "Joy to the World.") Sing up and down the scale again, singing letter names: "C, D, E..." Sing up and down a third time, singing the names of the syllables: "Do, Re, Mi..." Now you will see the connections between Maria's song and these tones, which are called a **C major scale.**

The C major scale is written like this, using alternate lines and spaces of a musical staff:

In the back of this book there is a chart of piano keys labeled with their names. You can use this as a guide and play a C major scale on a real keyboard. To find the starting note, look for a group of two black keys; the white key to their left is a C. Start there and play the white keys in order from left to right until you reach the next C; you will hear an ascending scale. Play them again from right to left; you will hear a descending scale. You can sing along and call these notes either by their letter names or by their syllables.

The distance between two neighboring notes is called a **scale step,** but not all steps are equal. Some pairs of white keys are separated by a black key, but other pairs are not separated by a black key because they already sound as close to each other as notes can sound in our musical system. The smallest distance between notes is called a **half step;** it is the distance between adjacent keys, whether white or black. Most scale steps are a **whole step** apart, which is the distance between two keys that have another one, white or black, between them.

*Do* is at both the bottom and the top of our scale because the series repeats itself both upward and downward, as high and as low as your ear can hear. Below every *Do* there is a *Ti,* and above every *Do* there is a *Re.*

What is the relationship between the lower *Do* and the higher one? They are different notes, but they sound so much alike that they have the same name. Why? The vibrations of the upper *Do* are exactly twice as fast as those of the lower one. If you play them together, every second vibration of the upper *Do* will coincide with a vibration of the lower *Do.* (You don't hear separate vibrations because they are much too fast. See the frequencies of various C's on page 78.) The distance between the two *Do's* is an **octave** (Latin *octo,* eight). In a voice class it is important to realize that women and men usually sing an octave apart. If women sing **in unison,** they all sing the same notes at the same time. If we say that a mixed group of people are singing in unison, this overlooks the fact that women and men are actually singing an octave apart. When men sing the songs in this book, they sound an octave lower than the notes are written. (Tenors in choir also sing an octave lower than their music is written.) If your teacher is of the opposite sex from you, you may need some practice before you can recognize and sing back the pitches that she or he sings for you.

Sometimes singers change a song, moving notes an octave higher or an octave lower than written either to add excitement to the song or to avoid problem tones.

Whole steps and half steps are also known as **seconds,** and the other **intervals** (distances between notes) have simple numerical names: a third, a fourth, etc. Each interval has its distinctive sound, and with practice you can learn to recognize them, but it is not necessary right now. For the present, you may learn your songs "by rote," that is, by hearing them repeatedly.

## Keys

Suppose a student asks, "What key is good for my voice?" First, we have to talk about what "in a key" means and the difference between the concepts of **key** and **range.**

Most pieces of music reach a point of finality at the end. If the piece were interrupted, you would be dissatisfied. Test this by asking someone to play any well-known tune on the piano and stop without playing the last note. There is a sense of incompleteness, even frustration.

To say that a song is in the key of C means that because we hear tones of the C major scale throughout the song we expect to hear the note C and a C chord at the end. A final tone expected in this way is called the **tonic,** and the chord built on it is called the **tonic chord.** A good example is "Do-Re-Mi," which fits this description exactly.

We intuitively grasp this system, called **tonality** or the **tonal system,** because we have heard thousands of pieces of music written in it.

Test this concept again by having the same song played with a "wrong" chord at the end!

Quite different from this is the concept of range, the distance between the lowest and highest notes of a song. Most people are comfortable singing "Do-Re-Mi" in the key of C. If it is too low for you, you might rather sing it in D major or E major. To change the key of a piece is called transposing it, and singers often transpose a song either up or down.

The tonic note of a song is not necessarily the lowest or the highest note of the song. And songs that are in your comfortable range are not necessarily all in the same key.

This is why the student's question mentioned earlier could not be answered easily. Two songs may be in the same key and yet have different ranges. What the student really wants to know is "Will the range of this song fit my voice?"

## Major scales

The C major scale is a useful model because its notes are played using only white keys on the keyboard. Also, its notes correspond to the lines and spaces of the musical staff without any added symbols. But the notes of C major are not the only ones in our musical system. Other notes are used to enable us to sing in a variety of keys.

In the C major scale we noticed that there were half steps between notes 3 and 4 and notes 7 and 8. All other major scales have that same pattern. Even if you are unaware of this pattern, it causes you to recognize the tonic of a major key.

Here is an example: When a scale begins on F, notes 3 and 4 need to be a half step apart. Since note 3 is A, note 4 cannot be B, which is a whole step higher. It must be B-flat instead. Musical notation shows this by placing a symbol called a **flat** at the beginning of the piece; the flat changes every written B in the piece to a B-flat. An F scale looks like this:

F    G    A    B♭    C    D    E    F    E    D    C    B♭    A    G    F

Just as a flat sign lowers a note by a half step, a **sharp** sign raises a note by a half step. Some notes have more than one name. Each of the black keys on a keyboard has two names, a sharp name and a flat name. A-sharp (a half step higher than A) is written differently from B-flat (a half step lower than B) on the musical staff, but sounds exactly the same and is the same key on the piano.

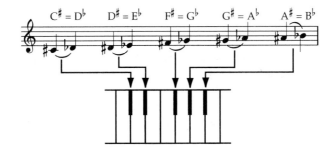

Since A-sharp (A♯) and B-flat (B♭) sound exactly the same when played on the piano, why do they have different names? Because they occur in the context of different scales, which are confusing to read if they are not written systematically.

The seven tones of C major plus the five tones that are played by black keys make a total of twelve tones in every octave. Played in order, the twelve tones form the **chromatic scale.** Any of the twelve can serve as the tonic of a key. This tonal system is typical of **Western music,** defined as the dominant artistic music of Western Europe and the Western Hemisphere. Other cultures—for instance, Chinese and Hindu—have evolved other musical systems with their own special features.

The great strength of Western music is the flexibility of tonal music. We can even change key, or **modulate,** in the middle of a song, meaning that the ear can be fooled into accepting a new note as a temporary tonic. This is achieved by the use of temporary alterations of the scale, called "chromatics." When you see flats or sharps in a piece of music, something like this may be going on. If you take a course in harmony, you will learn more about this.

**Minor scales**

So far we have not mentioned **minor keys,** but they have great charm and are not always sad, as people often think. To hear a minor scale, go back to the keyboard and play a scale on white keys from A to A. This is called the natural minor scale of A minor, and its most important feature is the half step between notes 2 and 3 (rather than 3 and 4 as in a major scale). Notes 6 and 7 are flexible in minor scales, often being raised a half step at the composer's wish.

## Looking at music

Even if you think you "can't read music," you can learn a lot by taking a close look at a song you want to learn in order to see what the printed page can tell you. As an example, let's use Cottrau's "Santa Lucia" on page 172. Before you begin to sing the song you will want to find out what it means by reading the English translation at the foot of the page and by reading the notes about the song on pages 293 and 294.

Just below the Italian title of the song is a small musical staff that shows the voice range of the song. Slightly lower down are two names, on the left the poet who wrote the words and on the right the composer of the music.

On the page are four **systems,** each made up of lines of music that are connected to each other by vertical lines at the left. Each line of music is written on a **staff** of five parallel lines. The first system does not contain a voice part because the voice does not sing during the piano introduction. In each of the other systems, the voice part is on the upper staff and the piano plays from the lower two staves, which are connected by the measure bars. Usually, the pianist's right hand plays from the upper staff and the left hand from the lower one, but crossovers also occur.

At the left of the upper one or two staves are fancy symbols called **G clefs,** which curl around the second line from the bottom; notes on this line are G's. The lowest staff has an **F clef,** formed of a curlicue and two dots to draw attention to the fourth line; notes on this line are F's. The midpoint between the upper and lower staves is **middle C,** which is written on a partial line, or *ledger line,* either below the upper staff or above the lower staff.

Immediately after the clefs there may be flat or sharp signs called the **key signature;** as explained previously, they show what key the music is in. The key signature is repeated on every line. The higher key of "Santa Lucia" (page 172) has no signature because it is in C, but the lower key (page 174) has three sharps because it is in the key of A.

Next comes a **meter signature** or **time signature,** in this case three over eight, or "three-eight time." The upper number means that there are three beats per measure, and the lower number shows that each beat is an eighth note. Aside from numbers, two other symbols may be used: C, meaning four-four time, and C with a slash, meaning two-two time.

"Santa Lucia" begins with an eight-measure piano introduction. At the end of m. 8 is a double bar line; later you will come back to this point and sing the music over again, using the words of the second stanza. In some other songs double repeat bars are used to show more complicated repeat patterns.

How will you get your first note? Notice that the piano plays your melody at the beginning of the introduction. The introduction also gives you plenty of time to feel the rhythm and tempo that will continue when you sing.

Once the voice begins to sing, there are no written rests to show where you can take a breath. In this song the punctuation marks are a reliable guide. Measures 9–12 are sung in one breath; breathe on the third beat of m. 12 so that you can sing on time in m. 13. You can also breathe in m. 15 and m. 17, and the pattern is clear from there on. Sometimes it is harder to decide about phrasing, and one has to decide whether to phrase according to the text meaning or the musical pattern.

After the first stanza the piano goes on playing. Measures 41–44 function as an **interlude** between the stanzas and also as a **postlude** after the second stanza.

Some folk and pop songs in this book have symbols above the vocal line to tell a pianist or guitarist what chords to play. The player decides how to play the chords, and it is not considered important for the notes to be exactly the same for every performance. In classical music chord symbols are not used because the composer has written the notes of the accompaniment with care, expecting them always to be the same.

This introduction to musical scores may raise more questions in your mind than it answers. But you can see that the score is a kind of roadmap, a chart from which you can get useful information even if you do not play an instrument.

If this chapter has awakened your curiosity, you would enjoy learning more in a course on rudiments of music or a beginning piano class.

### Additional reading

*For a clear, readable, thoroughly practical explanation of music symbols, based on tunes you already know:*

*Learn to Read Music* by Howard Shanet. Simon and Schuster, 1956.

## Melodies for note reading

The short melodies on the following pages begin very simply. Each new melody introduces one or two new factors, usually in a way that you can understand easily on the basis of the facts you already know.

Practice rhythms first, keeping regular time as you learned to do in chapters 5 and 9.

When you understand the rhythms, sing the pitches. The first melodies begin on F, but you may start on any pitch that is comfortable if you are practicing without a piano. The first melodies begin on the first note of the scale, called the tonic, or *do*.

In singing a melody it is important to recognize the up and down movement between the notes, regardless of the size of the step or leap. It may be helpful to sing the words "start," "up," "down," and "same" to keep track of direction. For instance, this is how you would sing "The Star-Spangled Banner": "Start, down, down, up, up, up, (breath) up, down, down, down, up, up (breath) same, same, up . . ."

Singing on la-la-la may be comfortable, but you will find that you sing more accurately if you sing a different name for each pitch. There are several good ways to do this. (If you are in a music school, the theory program of your school probably prefers one way over another.) The most common ways are to sing:

- Note names: F–G–A;
- Scale note numbers: 1–2–3; or
- Syllables with *do* on the tonic: Do-Re-Mi.

Another way, less common in America but favored by European musicians, is to call the note C by the name *Do* always, regardless of key.

Sing each melody over until you are confident that you have it right. This is called "sight-singing," but you may not get every melody right the first time. It is all right to practice.

It is also all right to follow the notes with your finger, even though you learned in school to read without doing so. And it is OK to label the notes with their names, whether you use F–G–A, 1–2–3, or d-r-m until you gain enough confidence to do without the labels.

# Melodies for Note Reading

13. Key of C

do  ti  la  so          fa  mi  re  do

14.

ti

15. Dotted rhythm in 3/4 meter
[1  (2) & 3]

16. Dotted rhythm on beat 2
[1  2  (3) &]

17. 3/8 meter (sounds the same as no. 16)

18. 6/8 meter (variation of no. 17)
[1  2  (3) & 4  (5)  6]

19. The same notes written with beams

20. Tie          [1  2  3  4  5]

21. Key of G, syncopation          [1  2  (3)  4]

do  mi  re  do  ti  la  so

22. Leap of a 5th

re  so

23. Leap of a 6th

so  ti

24. Chord outlines in a melody

do  mi  so          re  ti  so

# Songs

## America the Beautiful

CD 1 Track 40

Katherine Lee Bates

Samuel A. Ward

## Auld Lang Syne

CD 1 Track 41

Traditional

Scotland

Notes about these songs are on pages 283–284.

CD 1 Track 42

# Come, Follow!
## (a round)

John Hilton, adapted                                    John Hilton, adapted

**1** Come, fol - low, fol - low, fol - low, fol - low, fol - low, fol - low me!

**2** Whith-er shall I fol - low, fol - low, fol - low, whith-er shall I fol - low, fol - low thee?

**3** To the green - wood, to the green - wood, to the green - wood, green - wood tree.

CD 1 Track 43

# De colores

Traditional                                                    Mexico

De co - lo - res, de co - lo - res se vis - ten los cam - pos en la pri - ma - ve - ra; De co - lo - res, de co - lo - res son los pa - ja - ri - llos que vie - nen de fue - ra. De co - lo - res, de co - lo - res es el ar - co - i - ris que ve - mos lu - cir, y por e - so los gran - des a - mo - res de mu - chos co - lo - res me gus - tan a mí. Y por mí.

*Literal translation: With colors the fields are dressed in the springtime, and also the birds that come from afar, the rainbow that shines above. That's why I have a great love for bright colors.*

Notes about these songs are on page 284.

# Do-Re-Mi

CD 1 Track 44

Oscar Hammerstein II

Richard Rodgers

Doe, a deer, a fe - male deer, Ray, a drop of gol - den sun, _____

Me, a name I call my - self, Far, a long, long way to run, _____

Sew, a nee - dle pull - ing thread, _____ La, a note to fol - low sew, _____

Tea, a drink with jam and bread _____ that will bring us back to

do - oh - oh - oh! do! _____ Do - re - mi - fa - so - la - ti - do! _____

# Greeting Song

CD 1 Track 45

Traditional

Ghana

La - i - a - la - o - leh, sa - lam a - leh - kum! Li - a - la - o - leh!

**Solo:**                    **All:**

La - i - a - la - o - leh, Sa - lam a - leh - kum li - a - la - o - leh!

*"Salam alehkum" is Arabic for "Peace be with you," a common greeting. The other syllables have no meaning. The lower part is optional. The four-measure melody is sung many times, accompanied by bell and drums, while everyone greets everyone else. The second four measures are a variation to be used spontaneously when someone wants to lead the way. Dancing is welcome. Many variations are possible, just as m. 8 is a variation of m. 4. Singers can feel free to add English words, such as "Have a lovely day today" or "Happy Birthday."*

Notes about these songs are on pages 284–285.

CD 1 Track 46

# He's Got the Whole World in His Hands

Traditional

Spiritual

1. He's got the whole _____ world ___ in His hands, _ He's got the
2. He's got the wind and the rain ___ in His hands, _ He's got the
3. He's got the gamb - lin' ____ man ___ in His hands, _ He's got the

big, round ___ world _ in His hands, _ He's got the wide _____ world _
moon and the stars ___ in His hands, _ He's got the wind and the rain ___
ly - in' ___ man ___ in His hands, _ He's got the crap - shoot - in' man ___

(all stanzas)
in His hands, ___ He's got the whole world in His hands.

4. He's got the little-bitsy baby in His hands . . . (sing three times)

5. He's got you and me, brother, in His hands,
   He's got you and me, sister, in His hands,
   He's got you and me, brother, in His hands . . .

6. Oh, He's got everybody in His hands . . . (sing three times)

CD 1 Track 47

# Hinay Ma Tov
## (a round)

Psalm 133

Israel

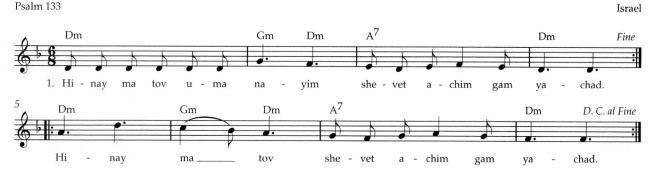

1. Hi - nay ma tov u - ma na - yim she - vet a - chim gam ya - chad.

Hi - nay ma _____ tov she - vet a - chim gam ya - chad.

*Literal translation: See how good and pleasant it is for brothers to dwell together!*

Notes about these songs are on page 285.

# Let There Be Peace on Earth

CD 1 Track 48

Sy Miller and Jill Jackson

Sy Miller and Jill Jackson

Notes about this song are on page 285.

CD 1 Track 49

# Scarborough Fair

Traditional                                                                                    England

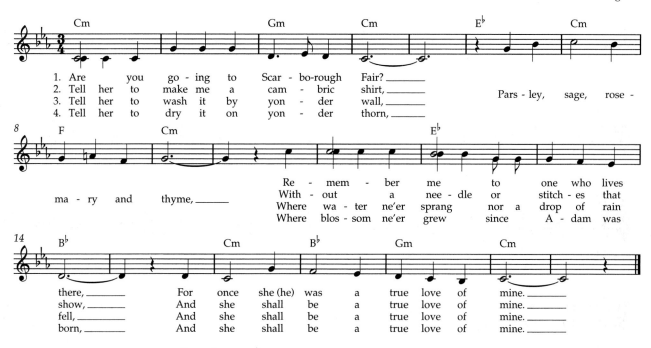

1. Are you go-ing to Scar-bo-rough Fair?_____ Pars-ley, sage, rose-
2. Tell her to make me a cam-bric shirt,_____
3. Tell her to wash it by yon-der wall,_____
4. Tell her to dry it on yon-der thorn,_____

ma-ry and thyme,_____
Re - mem - ber me to one who lives
With - out a nee - dle or stitch - es that
Where wa - ter ne'er sprang nor a drop of rain
Where blos - som ne'er grew since A - dam was

there,_____ For once she (he) was a true love of mine._____
show,_____ And she shall be a true love of mine._____
fell,_____ And she shall be a true love of mine._____
born,_____ And she shall be a true love of mine._____

Text when sung by a woman:

2. Tell him to bring me an acre of land, Parsley . . .
   Betwixt the wild ocean and yonder sea sand, And he . . .

3. Tell him to plough it with one ram's horn, Parsley . . .
   And sow it all over with one peppercorn, And he . . .

4. Tell him to reap it with a sickle of leather, Parsley . . .
   And bind it together with one peacock feather, And he . . .

CD 1 Track 50

# Sing and Rejoice!
## (a round)

Sing and re - joice, sing and re - joice!

Let all things liv - ing____ now____ sing and re - joice!

Notes about these songs are on page 285.

# The Star-Spangled Banner

CD 1 Track 51

Francis Scott Key

John Stafford Smith

Notes about this song are on page 285.

CD 1 Track 52

# This Little Light of Mine

Traditional

Spiritual

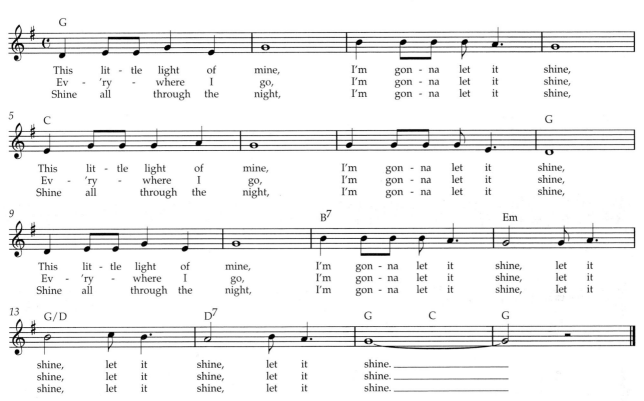

CD 1 Track 53

# Viva la musica!

## (a round)

Traditional

Michael Praetorius

*Literal translation: Long live music!*

Notes about these songs are on page 285.

# All the Notes of All the Earth

CD 1 Track 54

John Russell
Second stanza by J. G. P.

Hungary
*Arranged by Ralph R. Whitehead*

1. All the notes of all the earth make one great song:
2. We can let our voic-es join that one great song,

Pas-sion, sor-row, all the cries of right and wrong,
Let our joys and long-ings ring out loud and strong—

All that has been, all that is, and yet shall be,
Songs of mem'-ry, songs of love that yet shall be,

Notes about this song are on page 286.

They who lis - ten hear as one great har - mo - ny.
They who lis - ten hear as one great har - mo - ny.

# Auprès de ma blonde

CD 1 Track 55

Traditional

Normandy, France
*Arranged by J. G. P.*

1. Au jar - din de mon pè - re Les
2. La caill', la tour - te - rel - le Et
3. Ell' chan - te pour les fil - les Qui

*mf*

*p*

lau - riers sont fleu - ris; _____ Au jar - din de mon pè - re Les
la jo - lie per - drix, _____ La caill', la tour - te - rel - le, Et
n'ont point de ma - ri; _____ Ell' chan - te pour les fil - les Qui

lau - riers sont fleu - ris; _____ Tous les oi - seaux du mon - de Vont
la jo - lie per - drix _____ Et la blan - che co - lom - be Qui
n'ont point de ma - ri; _____ C'est pas pour moi qu'ell' chan - te, Car

*Literal translation:* (1) *In my father's garden / the laurels are blooming; / birds from everywhere / go there to nest . . .*
(2) *The quail, the turtledove, / the pretty partridge, / and the white dove, / which sings day and night . . .*
(3) *The dove sings for the girls / who have no husbands, / but it does not sing for me, / because I have a handsome one.*

Notes about this song are on page 286.

*(Refrain) Beside my blonde wife, / how good it is to sleep!*

# Carmela

Traditional

CD 1 Track 56

Mexico

*Arranged by J. G. P.*

*Literal translation: (1) Just as the sun's rays fade in the west, so my dreams are dying.*
*(2) Precious pearl of my love, how can flowers compare to you? Looking at them one by one, not one is as beautiful as you.*

Notes about this song are on page 287.

*Carmen, dear Carmen, light of my eyes, if there were no other light, you would be light for me.*
*Lovely lamp of good fortune, sweet hope, lovely happiness.*

108

*(High Key)*

# Cielito lindo

Traditional

CD 1 Track 57

Mexico
*Arranged by J. G. P.*

1. De la Sie - rra Mo - re - na vie - nen ba - jan - do, vie -
2. Pa - ja - ro___ que a-ban - do - na su___ pri - mer ni - do, su___
3. E - se lu - nar que tie - nes, cie - li - to lin - do, jun -

- nen ba - jan - do,___ Un par de o - ji - tos
___ pri - mer ni - do,___ Re - gre - sa___ y ya no en -
- to a la bo - ca,___ No se lo___ des a

ne - gros, cie - li - to lin - do, de___ con - tra - ban - do.___
cuen - tra, cie - li - to lin - do, el___ bien per - di - do.___
na - die, cie - li - to lin - do, que a___ mi me to - ca.___

*Literal translation: (1) From the high mountains a pair of dark eyes came down to me, beautiful darling! precious eyes!*
*(2) The bird that leaves its first nest and then goes back does not find its lost love again.*
*(3) That beauty mark that you have near your mouth, don't give it to anyone; it belongs to me.*

Notes about this song are on page 287–288.

*(Low Key)*

# Cielito lindo

Traditional

Mexico

*Arranged by J. G. P.*

1. De la Sie - rra Mo - re - na vie - nen ba - jan - do, vie -
2. Pa - ja - ro___ que a-ban - do - na su___ pri - mer ni - do, su -
3. E - se lu - nar que tie - nes, cie - li - to lin - do, jun -

- nen ba - jan - do,_____ Un par de o - ji - tos
___ pri - mer ni - do,_____ Re - gre - sa___ y ya no en -
- to a la bo - ca,_____ No se lo___ des a

ne - gros, cie - li - to lin - do, de___ con - tra - ban - do._____
cuen - tra, cie - li - to lin - do, el___ bien per - di - do._____
na - die, cie - li - to lin - do, que a mi me to - ca._____

*Literal translation: (1) From the high mountains a pair of dark eyes came down to me, beautiful darling! precious eyes!*
*(2) The bird that leaves its first nest and then goes back does not find its lost love again.*
*(3) That beauty mark that you have near your mouth, don't give it to anyone; it belongs to me.*

Notes about this song are on page 287–88.

# Deep River

CD 1 Track 59

Traditional

Spiritual
*Arranged by Henry Thacker Burleigh*

Deep _____ riv - er, my home is o - ver Jor - dan, _____ Deep _____ riv - er, Lord, I want to cross o - ver in - to camp ground.

Notes about this song are on page 288.

prom - is'd land __ where all __ is

peace? Oh, deep _____ riv - er, Lord, I

want to cross o - ver in - to camp ground. ___

This page is intentionally left blank
to provide better page turns in
the succeeding songs.

# Down by the Salley Gardens

William Butler Yeats

Ireland
*Arranged by Herbert Hughes*

CD 1 Track 60

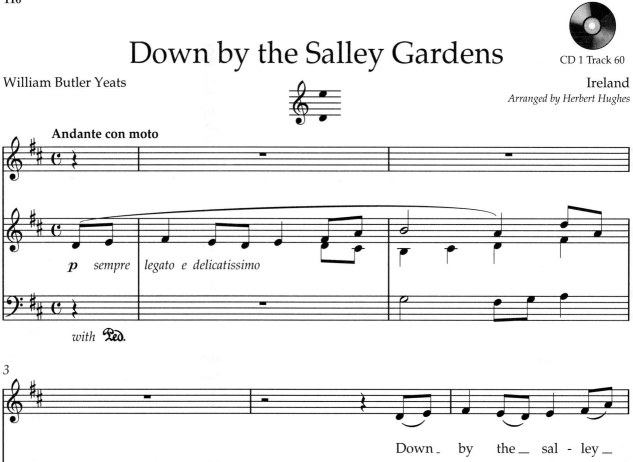

Copyright 1909 by Boosey & Hawkes

Notes about this song are on page 288.

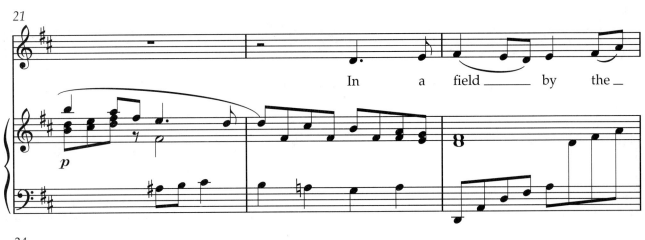

In a field ____ by the ____

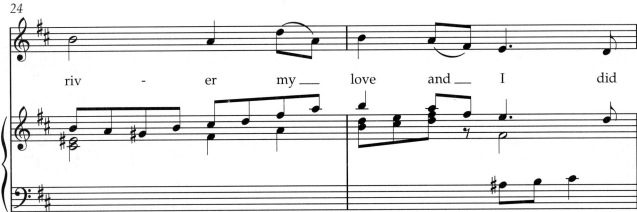

riv - er my ____ love and ____ I did

stand, And ____ on my ____ lean - ing shoul - der she ____

laid her ____ snow - white hand. She bid me ____ take life

ea - sy, as the grass grows_ on _ the_ weirs; But _____

I was_ young and_ fool - ish and_ now am_ full of

tears. _____

# Drink to Me Only with Thine Eyes

CD 1 Track 61

Ben Jonson

England

*Arranged by Roger Quilter*

Notes about this song are on page 288.

thine.

I sent thee late a ro - sy wreath,_ Not so_ much honour-ing

thee, _____ As giv-ing it a hope _ that there _ It

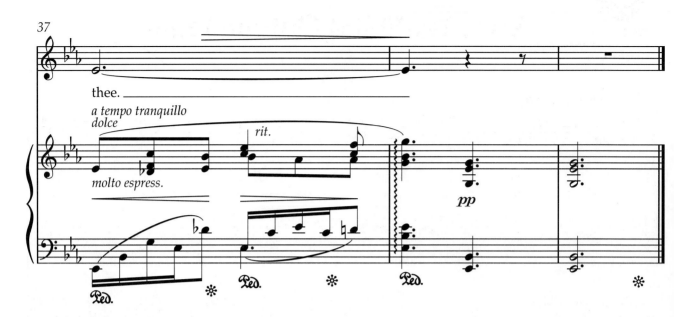

thee.

*a tempo tranquillo*
*dolce*

*rit.*

*molto espress.*

*pp*

Ped. ✻ Ped. ✻ Ped.  ✻

# Love Will Find Out the Way

Traditional

England
*Arranged by J. G. P.*

Notes about this song are on page 288.

10
deepest, Which __ Nep - tune o - bey, O - ver
venture, Lest her - self fast she __ lay, If __

13
rocks that are __ steep - est, Love will find out the
love come he will en - ter And soon find out his

16
way.
way.
Some think to __

19
lose him By __ hav - ing him con - fined,

# Sakura, Sakura

CD 1 Track 63

Traditional

Japan
*Arranged by J.G.P.*

*Literal translation: Cherry blossoms! Look around at the March sky, mists or clouds. Fragrance is coming. Let's go to look!*

Notes about this song are on page 288.

Ni - o - i zo i - zu - ru, I - za - ya,

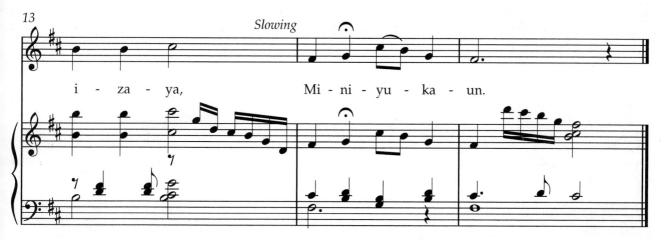

i - za - ya, Mi - ni - yu - ka - un.

# The Turtle Dove

Traditional

English Folk Song
*Arranged by V. A. C.*

CD 1 Track 64

**Andante sostenuto**

*pp* 1. Fare - well, my dear, I    must be __ gone, And __ leave you __ for a -
*mp* 2. So __    fair thou art, my    bon - ny __ lass, So __ deep in __ love am __
*mf* 3. The __    crow that's black, my    lit-tle tur-tle dove, Shall __ change its __ col - ors __

while;    For __ though __ I __ go  I'll __ come    back a - gain, Though I
I;    But I    nev - er    will prove false to the    bon - ny lass I love, Till the
white    Be - fore __    I am false to the    one __ that I love, The __

Notes about this song are on page 288.

*(High Key)*

# It Was a Lover and His Lass

CD 1 Track 65

William Shakespeare

Thomas Morley
*Arranged by J. G. P.*

1. It was a lov-er and his lass, With a hay, and a ho, and a hay no-ni-no, and a hay ___ no-ni-no-ni no. That

2. This car-ol they be-gan that hour, With a hay, and a ho, and a hay no-ni-no, and a hay ___ no-ni-no-ni no. How

Notes about this song are on page 289.

spring. In spring - time, in spring -
time, the on - ly pret - ty ring - time, When
birds do sing, Hay ding-a-ding-a-ding, hay ding-a-ding-a-ding, hay
ding-a-ding-a-ding, Sweet lov - ers love the spring!

*(Low Key)*

# It Was a Lover and His Lass

William Shakespeare

Thomas Morley
*Arranged by J. G. P.*

Notes about this song are on page 289.

*(High Key)*

# Since First I Saw Your Face

Thomas Ford

Thomas Ford
*Realization by J. G. P.*

CD 1 Track 67

*Lyrics:*

Since first I saw your face I re-solved To hon - or and re - nown ____ you. If now I be dis - dained, I ____ wish my heart had nev - er known ____ you. What, I that loved and

If I ad-mire or praise you too much, That fault you may for - give ____ me. Or if my hands had strayed but a touch, Then just - ly might you leave ____ me. I asked you leave, you

Notes about this song are on page 289.

you that liked, Shall we be - gin to wran - gle? No, no,
bade me love, Is now the time to chide me? No, no,

no, my heart is fast, And can - not dis - en - tan - gle.
no, I'll love you still What for - tune e'er be - tide me.

*(Low Key)*

# Since First I Saw Your Face

Thomas Ford

CD 1 Track 68

Thomas Ford
*Realization by J. G. P.*

Since first I saw your face I re-solved To hon - or and re-
If I ad-mire or praise you too much, That fault you may for-

nown _____ you. If now I be dis - dained, I _____ wish my
give _____ me. Or if my hands had strayed but a touch, Then

heart had nev - er known _____ you. What, I that loved and
just - ly might you leave _____ me. I asked you leave, you

Notes about this song are on page 289.

you that liked, Shall we be - gin to wran - gle? No, no,
bade me love, Is now the time to chide me? No, no,

no, my heart is fast, And can - not dis - en - tan - gle.
no, I'll love you still What for - tune e'er be - tide me.

*(High Key)*

# The Silver Swan

Anonymous

Orlando Gibbons
*Arranged by J.G.P.*

CD 1 Track 69

The sil - ver swan, who liv - ing had no note, When death ap-proached un - locked her si - lent throat. Lean - ing her breast a - gainst the reed - y shore, Thus sung her first and

Notes about this song are on page 289.

last and _ sung no more: "Fare - well, all

joys! Oh Death, come close mine eyes! More

geese than swans now live, more _ fools than wise."

*rit.*

*(Low Key)*

# The Silver Swan

Anonymous

Orlando Gibbons
*Arranged by J.G.P.*

CD 1 Track 70

The sil - ver swan, who liv - ing had no note, When

death ap-proached un - locked her si - lent throat. Lean - ing her

breast a - gainst the reed - y shore, Thus sung her first and

Notes about this song are on page 289.

last and _ sung no more: "Fare - well, all

joys! Oh Death, come close mine eyes! More

geese than swans now live, more _ fools than wise."

*rit.*

*(High Key)*

# Dolce scherza

Anonymous

Giacomo Antonio Perti
*Realization by J. G. P.*

CD 1 Track 71

*Literal translation: A lovely mouth sweetly teases and sweetly smiles, breathing love.*

Notes about this song are on page 290.

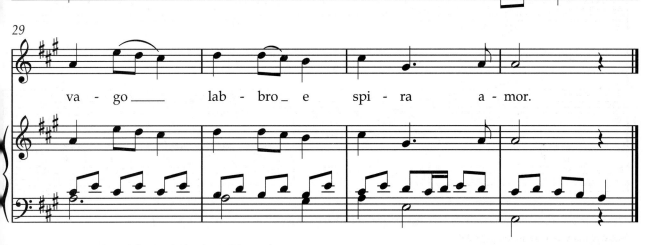

*But it pleases you and then kills you; that's what it did to my heart.*

*(Low Key)*

# Dolce scherza

CD 1 Track 72

Anonymous

Giacomo Antonio Perti

*Realization by J. G. P.*

*Literal translation: A lovely mouth sweetly teases and sweetly smiles, breathing love.*

Notes about this song are on page 290.

But it pleases you and then kills you; that's what it did to my heart.

*(High Key)*

# Io le dirò che l'amo

Silvio Stampiglia

George Frideric Handel

CD 1 Track 73

*Literal translation: I will tell her that I love her and I will not be fearful.*

Notes about this song are on pages 290–291.

*And because I desire her for my own, I know what I must do.*

*(Low Key)*

# Io le dirò che l'amo

Silvio Stampiglia

George Frideric Handel

CD 1 Track 74

*Literal translation: I will tell her that I love her and I will not be fearful.*

Notes about this song are on pages 290–291.

*And because I desire her for my own, I know what I must do.*

*(High Key)*

# Sigh No More, Ladies

William Shakespeare

Richard J. S. Stevens
*Arranged by J. L. Hatton and E. Faning*

CD 1 Track 75

**Allegretto**

Sigh no more, la - dies, la - dies, sigh no more, ___
Sing no more, la - dies, la - dies, sing no more ___ Of

Men were de-ceiv-ers ev - er, men were de-ceiv-ers ev - er;
dumps so ___ dull and heav-y, of dumps so ___ dull and heav-y;

One foot in sea and one ___ on shore, ___ To
The fraud of men was ev - er so, ___ Since

Notes about this song are on page 292.

non - ny,      hey   non - ny,    non - ny,      hey    non - ny,

non-ny,      hey   non-ny,   non-ny!

# Sigh No More, Ladies

*(Low Key)*

William Shakespeare

Richard J. S. Stevens
*Arranged by J. L. Hatton and E. Faning*

**Allegretto**

Sigh no more, la - dies, la - dies, sigh no more, ____
Sing no more, la - dies, la - dies, sing no more ____ Of

Men were de-ceiv - ers ev - er, men were de-ceiv - ers ev - er;
dumps so ___ dull and heav - y, of dumps so ___ dull and heav - y;

One foot in sea and one _____ on shore, ___ To
The fraud of men was ev - er so, _____ Since

Notes about this song are on page 292.

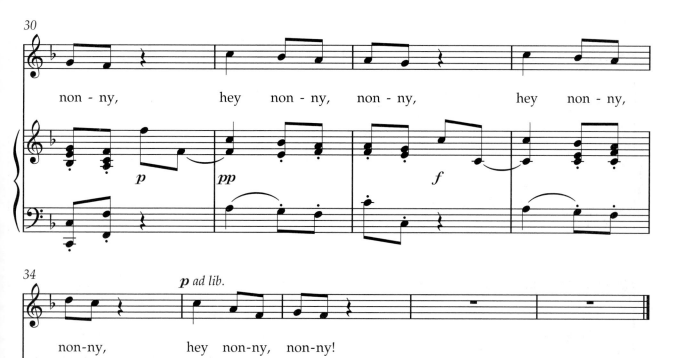

non - ny,       hey  non - ny,   non - ny,      hey   non - ny,

non-ny,      hey  non-ny,  non-ny!

*(High Key)*

# Bitten

### Prayer

CD 1 Track 77

Christian Fürchtegott Gellert
*Translation by V. A. C. and J. G. P.*

Ludwig van Beethoven

**Feierlich und mit Andacht**
*Solemnly, and with devotion*

Gott, dei - ne Gü - te reicht _ so weit, So weit die
O God, your good - ness reach - es far, As far as

Wol - ken ge - hen; Du krönst uns mit Barm - her - zig -
clouds a - bove us; Your love ac - cepts us as we

*Literal translation: God, your goodness reaches / as far as the clouds. / You crown us with your mercy /*

Notes about this song are on page 292.

*and hurry to support us. | Lord, my fortress, my rock, my protection, | hear my pleading, heed my words, | because I want to pray to you.*

*(Low Key)*

# Bitten

### Prayer

CD 2 Track 1

Christian Fürchtegott Gellert
*Translation by V. A. C. and J. G. P.*

Ludwig van Beethoven

**Feierlich und mit Andacht**
*Solemnly, and with devotion*

Gott, dei - ne Gü - te reicht _ so weit, So weit die
O God, your good - ness reach - es far, As far as

Wol - ken ge - hen; Du krönst uns mit Barm - her - zig -
clouds a - bove us; Your love ac - cepts us as we

*Literal translation: God, your goodness reaches / as far as the clouds. / You crown us with your mercy /*

Notes about this song are on page 292.

*and hurry to support us. / Lord, my fortress, my rock, my protection, / hear my pleading, heed my words, / because I want to pray to you.*

# Who Is Sylvia?

William Shakespeare

Franz Schubert

1. Who is Syl - via, what is she, ___ That all our swains com - mend her?
2. Is she kind ___ as she is fair? ___ For beau - ty lives with kind - ness:

Ho - ly,
Love doth

Notes about this song are on page 293.

dor - ed __ be.
hab - its __ there.

3. Then to

Syl - via let us sing, __ That

Syl - via is ex - cel - ing;

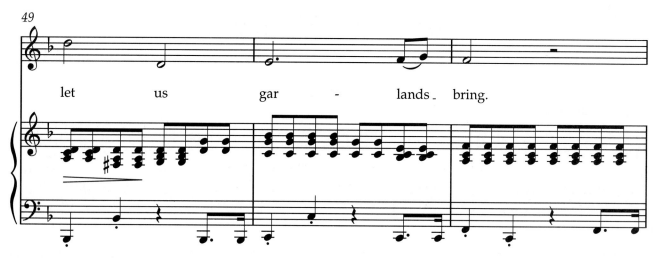

let          us          gar  -          lands ‿          bring.

# Beautiful Dreamer

Stephen C. Foster

Stephen C. Foster

Notes about this song are on page 293.

*(High Key)*

# Santa Lucia

CD 2 Track 4

Teodoro Cottrau

Teodoro Cottrau

Lyrics (voice line):

1. Sul ma - re luc-ci-ca
2. Con que - sto zef-fi-ro

L'a - stro d'ar-gen - to, Pla - ci - da è l'on - da, Pro - spe - ro è il
Co - sì so - a - ve, Oh! co - m'è bel - lo Star sul - la

ven - to. Sul ma - re luc-ci-ca L'a-stro d'ar-gen - to, Pla - ci - da è
na - ve! Con que - sto zef-fi-ro Co - sì so - a - ve Oh! co - m'è

*Literal translation: (1) On the sea shines a silver star; calm are the waves, favorable the wind.*
*(2) With this breeze so gentle, how lovely it is to be on a boat!*

Notes about this song are on pages 293–294.

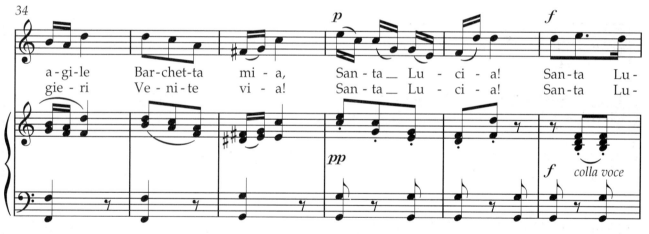

*(1) Come to my fine little boat, Santa Lucia!*
*(2) Come on, passengers! Let's go! Santa Lucia!*

*(Low Key)*

# Santa Lucia

CD 2 Track 5

Teodoro Cottrau

Teodoro Cottrau

*Literal translation: (1) On the sea shines a silver star; calm are the waves, favorable the wind.*
*(2) With this breeze so gentle, how lovely it is to be on a boat!*

Notes about this song are on pages 293–294.

(1) *Come to my fine little boat, Santa Lucia!*
(2) *Come on, passengers! Let's go! Santa Lucia!*

# Willow, Tit-Willow

CD 2 Track 6

William S. Gilbert

Arthur Sullivan

Andante espressivo ♩. = 63

1. On a tree by a riv - er a
2. He _ slapped at his chest, as he

lit - tle tom - tit    Sang, __ "Wil-low,    tit - wil-low,    tit - wil-low!" _    And I
sat on that bough,  Sing - ing "Wil-low,    tit - wil-low,    tit - wil-low!" _    And a

said to him "Dick-y-bird, why do you sit    Sing-ing 'Wil-low,    tit - wil-low,    tit -
cold per-spi - ra-tion be - span-gled his brow,    Oh, __ wil-low,    tit - wil-low,    tit -

Notes about this song are on page 294.

wil-low?" _ Is it weak-ness of in - tel-lect, bird-ie?" I cried, "Or a

wil-low! _ He _ sobbed and he sighed, and a gur-gle he gave, Then he

rath - er tough worm in your lit - tle in-side?" With a shake of his poor lit - tle

plunged him-self in - to the bil-low-y wave, And an ech - o a - rose from the

head he re - plied, "Oh, wil-low, tit - wil-low, tit - wil-low!" _

su - i-cide's grave– "Oh, wil-low, tit - wil-low, tit - wil-low!" _

3. Now I feel just as sure as I'm

_p_

sure that my name Is-n't Wil-low, tit-wil-low, tit-wil-low,_ That 'twas

blight-ed af-fec-tion that made him ex-claim, "Oh, wil-low, tit-wil-low, tit-

wil-low!"_ And if you re-main cal-lous and ob-du-rate, I Shall_

per-ish as he did, and you will know why, Though I prob-a-bly shall not ex-

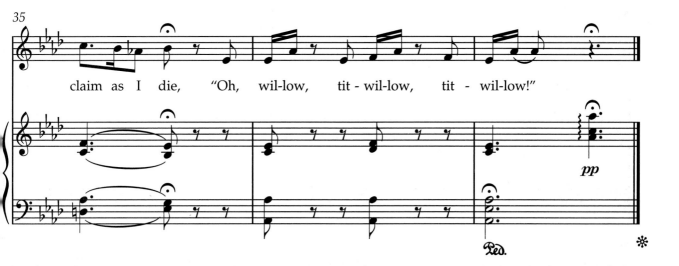

claim as I die, "Oh, wil-low, tit - wil-low, tit - wil-low!"

# In Haven

## (Capri)

CD 2 Track 7

C. A. Elgar

Edward Elgar

Close - ly let me hold thy hand;___ Storms are sweep - ing

sea and land;___

Notes about this song are on page 294.

Love a - lone will stand.

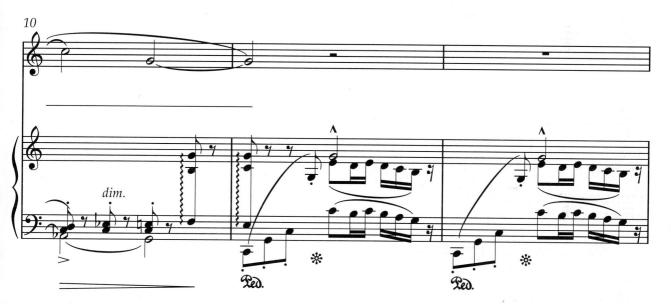

Close - ly cling, for waves beat fast,___ Foam flakes cloud the

hur - rying blast; _____ Love a - lone will

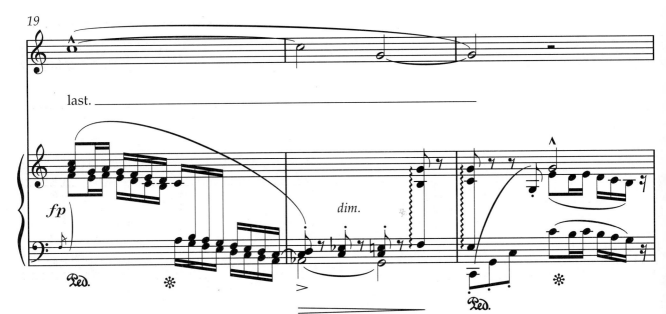

last. _____

Kiss my lips and soft - ly say, _____

"Joy, sea - swept, may fade to - day; _____

Love a - lone will stay." _____

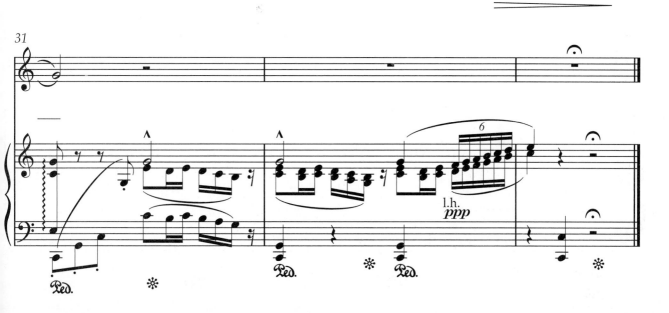

# E l'uccellino

Renato Fucini

Giacomo Puccini

CD 2 Track 8

*Literal translation: And the little bird sings on the branch: Sleep peacefully, little dear. Lay down your*

Notes about this song are on pages 294–295.

*fair head on mama's heart. And the little bird sings on the twig: So many nice things you will learn, but if you want to know how much I*

*love you, no one on earth can ever say it. And the little bird sings to the bright sky: Sleep, my treasure, here on my bosom.*

# The Sky above the Roof

Paul Verlaine
*Translated by Mabel Dearmer*

Ralph Vaughan Williams

The sky a - bove the

roof is calm and sweet: A tree a - bove the roof Bends \_\_\_

\_\_ in the heat. A bell from out the

Notes about this song are on page 296.

188

tears?     What hast thou done, O heart,_____ With thy spent _

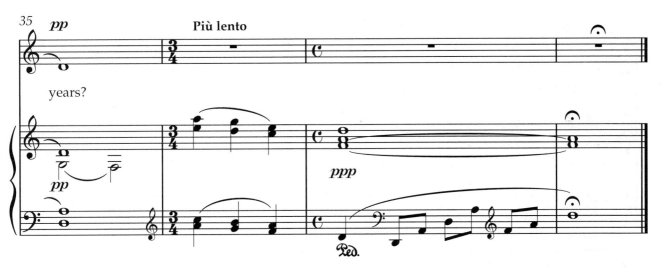

years?

Più lento

# Star-Eyes
## (Stjärnöga)

CD 2 Track 9

Bo Bergman
*English version by J.G.P.*

Wilhelm Stenhammar

Allegretto semplice

Star - Eyes, __ you were the light
Stjärn - ö - ga, du som jag mött

Shin - ing to guide me for - ward; Now it is
långt i för - svun - na ti - der, nu är det

twi - light, and yet With-out you I must go on - ward.
kväll - dags, och trött min ung - dom till vi - la skri - der.

*Literal translation: Star-Eyes, you whom I met far away and long ago, now night is coming and my young self has grown tired and wants to rest.*

Notes about this song are on pages 295–296.

16

Brief, bright il - lu - sions there are, Prom - is - ing
Irr - bloss, som värl - den har tänt, slock - na så

20

they can guide me, But they can - not be my star,
lätt i värl - den. Stjärn - ö - ga, myc - ket har hänt,

*espress.*

*dim.*

26

Since you are not here be - side me.
se - dan vi skil - des på fär - den.

*p*

*Illusions that the world has lighted up now disappear. Star-Eyes, much has happened since we said goodbye along the path.*

*Now a confusing road ahead passes through dark countries. Star-Eyes, will I never again hold your hands?   Take my*

*hands and lead me into your realm of light. Star-Eyes, give me your peace and let me become like you.*

# Serenity
### A unison chant

CD 2 Track 11

John Greenleaf Whittier

Charles Ives

Notes about this song are on page 296.

# Serenade

CD 2 Track 13

Robert Browning

Gena Branscombe

Notes about this song are on page 296.

# By the Sea

Roger Quilter

Roger Quilter

Notes about this song are on page 296.

199

# Fancy

William Shakespeare

Francis Poulenc

CD 2 Track 14

Tell me where is fan-cy bred, or in the heart, or in the head?

Now be-got, how nou-ri-shed? Re-ply, re-ply,

re-ply.___ It is en-gen-der'd in the eyes

Notes about this song are on page 296.

With ga-zing fed and fan-cy dies. In the cra - dle

where it lies. Let us all ring fan - cy's knell;

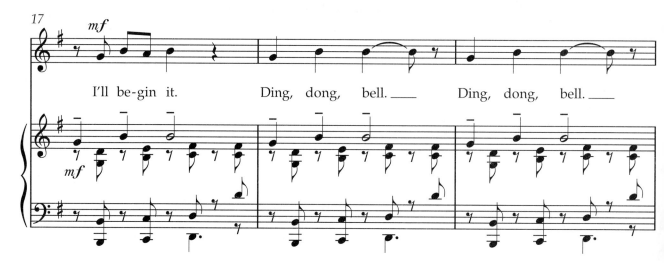

I'll be-gin it. Ding, dong, bell.___ Ding, dong, bell.___

Ding, dong, bell.          Ding, dong, bell.          Ding, dong, bell.

# Vos me matásteis

Traditional

Joaquin Rodrigo

CD 2 Track 15

*Literal translation: You have destroyed me, little one with hair hanging down. You have killed me.*

Notes about this song are on page 297.

*Literal translation: I saw you on the bank of a river, young virgin.*

de un ri - o, vi mo-za vir - gen, _____

ni - ña en ca-be - llo, _____ vos me ma-tás - teis,

ni - ña en _ ca-be-llo, __ vos me _ ha-béis muer - to, vos me_ ha-béis muer-to.

# The Lord Has a Child

CD 2 Track 16

Langston Hughes *

William Schuman

\* Text used by permission.

Notes about this song are on page 297.

209

all I ought to be, His lov-ing care guides me on my

way, Ev - 'ry place, ev - 'ry-where, ev - 'ry day. \_\_\_\_\_

*più mosso*

Wear - y this world, \_\_\_ Heav - y my load;

*poco rit.* *a tempo*

Bur - dens I bear \_ On this rock - y road, But the

*(High Key)*

CD 2 Track 17

# To a Brown Girl, Dead

Countee Cullen

Margaret Bonds

Notes about this song are on page 297.

Death has found her sweet. _____ Her

moth-er pawned her wed-ding ring _____ To lay her out _ in

white. _____ She'd be so proud she'd dance and sing To

see her-self _____ to - night. _____

(Low Key)

# To a Brown Girl, Dead

Countee Cullen

CD 2 Track 18

Margaret Bonds

Notes about this song are on page 297.

# A Song Without Words

(Based on the singing of Blind Willie Johnson)

Charles Brown

CD 2 Track 19

*Vocalize throughout on "ah" or hum.*

*Note heads that appear as ✗ in the voice part are simply "blue" note approximations.

Copyright © 1974 by Charles S. Brown.

Notes about this song are on page 297.

# Lo, How a Rose

Traditional

Hughes Huffman, Jr.

CD 2 Track 20

Notes about this song are on page 297.

# It Don't Mean a Thing

CD 2 Track 21

Irving Mills

Duke Ellington

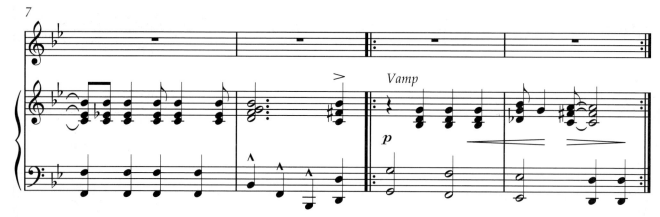

What good is mel-o-dy,＿ what good is mus-ic,＿

Notes about this song are on page 298.

222

(doo wah, \_ doo wah, doo wah, doo wah, doo wah, \_

\_ doo wah, doo wah, doo wah.) It don't mean a

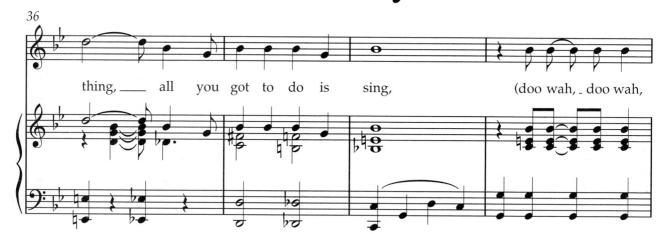

thing, \_ all you got to do is sing, (doo wah, \_ doo wah,

doo wah, doo wah, doo wah, \_ doo wah, doo wah, doo wah.) It

makes no diff-'rence if ___ it's sweet or hot, _____ Just

give that rhy-thm ev'-ry-thing you got, Oh, it don't mean a

thing, if it ain't got that swing, _ (doo wah, _ doo wah,

doo wah, doo wah, doo wah, _ doo wah, doo wah, doo wah.) It wah.)

(High Key)

# Love Is Here to Stay

Ira Gershwin

George Gershwin

CD 2 Track 22

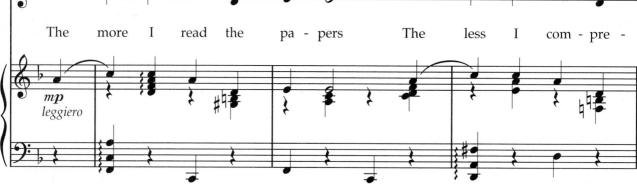

The more I read the pa-pers The less I com-pre-

hend The world and all its ca-pers And how it all will

Notes about this song are on page 298.

27

Not for a year, But ev - er and a day.

31

The ra - di - o and the tel - e-phone and the mov - ies that we

35

know May just be pass-ing fan - cies, And in time may go.

*cresc.*

*mf*

39

But, oh my dear, Our love is here to stay;

*p cresc.*

*(Low Key)*

# Love Is Here to Stay

Ira Gershwin

CD 2 Track 23

George Gershwin

Notes about this song are on page 298.

27

Not for a year, But ev - er and a day.

31

The ra - di - o and the tel - e-phone and the mov-ies that we

35

know May just be pass-ing fan - cies, And in time may go.

*cresc.*

*mf*

39

But, oh my dear, Our love is here to stay;

*p* *cresc.*

# Over the Rainbow

CD 2 Track 24

E. Y. Harburg

Harold Arlen

Notes about this song are on page 298.

# I'll Know

CD 2 Track 27

Frank Loesser

Frank Loesser

**Moderato**

*With expression*
*a tempo*

I'll know when my love comes a-long, I'll know then and

there. I'll know at the sight of ( her / his ) face How I

Notes about this song are on page 298.

stop      and I'll   stare      at that face      in   the

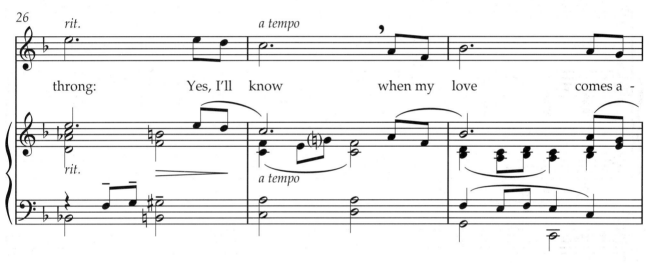

throng:      Yes, I'll    know      when my   love      comes a -

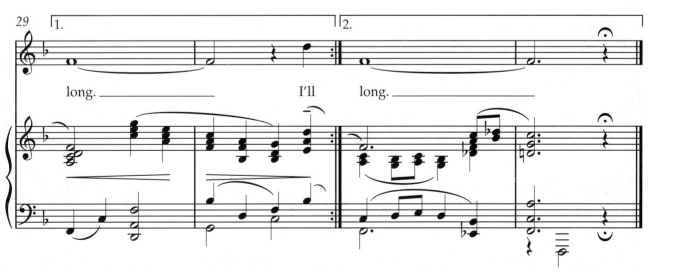

long._____      I'll      long._____

# They Say It's Wonderful

Irving Berlin

Irving Berlin

CD 2 Track 25

Notes about this song are on page 298.

# A Cockeyed Optimist

Oscar Hammerstein II

Richard Rodgers

CD 2 Track 26

Notes about this song are on page 298.

*(High Key)*

# One Hand, One Heart

Stephen Sondheim

Leonard Bernstein

CD 2 Track 28

Notes about this song are on page 298.

Make of our lives one life. Day af-ter day one

life. Now it be-gins, now we start; One hand,

one heart. E-ven death won't part_____ us now._____

now._____

*(Low Key)*

# One Hand, One Heart

CD 2 Track 29

Stephen Sondheim

Leonard Bernstein

Notes about this song are on page 298.

Make of our lives one life. Day af-ter day one

life. Now it be-gins, now we start; One hand,

one heart. E - ven death won't part us now.

now.

# Soon It's Gonna Rain

Tom Jones

Harvey Schmidt

CD 2 Track 30

Notes about this song are on page 298.

35 Soon it's gon-na rain. What-'ll we do with you

38 We'll find four limbs of a tree. We'll

41 build four walls and a floor. We'll bind it

44 o - ver with leaves And run in - side to stay.

*rit.*

CD 2 Track 31

# Make Someone Happy

Betty Comden and Adolph Green

Jule Styne

Make _____ some-one hap-py, make just one ___ some-one hap-py,

Make just one ___ heart the heart you sing to.

Notes about this song are on page 299.

# In My Life

CD 2 Track 32

John Lennon and Paul McCartney

John Lennon and Paul McCartney

**Moderately**

There are plac-es I'll re-mem-ber all my
But of all these friends and lov-ers there is

life, _____ though some have changed. \_ Some for-ev-er, not for
no \_\_\_\_\_ one com-pares with you. \_ And these mem-'ries lose their

bet-ter; some have gone _____ and some re-main. \_ All these
mean-ing when I think of \_ love as some-thing new. \_ Tho' I

Notes about this song are on page 299.

# Happiness

Clark Gesner

Clark Gesner

Notes about this song are on page 299.

Ty - ing your shoe for the ver - y first time. Hap-pi-ness is
Shar-ing a sand-wich, __ get-ting a - long. Hap-pi-ness is

play - ing the drum in your own school band. And
sing - ing to - geth - er when day is through. And

Hap-pi-ness is walk-ing hand in hand. _____
Hap-pi-ness is those who sing with you. _____

CD 2 Track 37

# Once upon a Dream

Leslie Bricusse

Frank Wildhorn

Notes about this song are on page 299.

dream, you were heav - en - sent to me.

But it was - n't meant to be, now you're just a dream.

Could we be - gin a-gain, once up-on a dream?

# Believe in Yourself

Charlie Smalls

Charlie Smalls

Notes about this song are on page 299.

you be - lieve, _____ I know you will. _____

Be - lieve in your-self right from the start;

you'll have brains, you'll have a heart. You'll have cour-age to

last your whole life through, _____ if you be -

lieve in your-self, _____ if you be - lieve in your-self, _____

\_\_\_ if you be - lieve in your-self as I be - lieve in

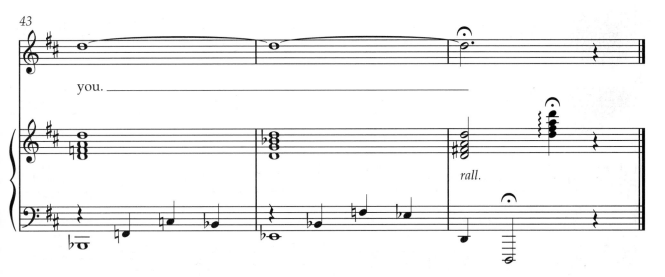

you. _____

rall.

# What I Did for Love

Edward Kleban

Marvin Hamlisch

Kiss to-day _ good-bye, _____

The sweet-ness and the sor-row. _____ We did what _ we

had to do, _____ And I can't re-gret _

Notes about this song are on page 299.

And point me t'ward to - mor-row. _____ Wish me luck, _ the

same to you. _____ Won't for-get, _

_ can't re - gret _ What I did _ for love,

What I did for _ love, What I did for _ love. _____

# In A Simple Way I Love You

Gretchen Cryer

Nancy Ford

CD 2 Track 36

Notes about this song are on page 299.

22

I'm here to see you through. I'll make mu-sic while you

25

sing your song while you do what you have to do.

28

I'll be be-side you rain or shine, Love has man-y fac-es, and

*poco a poco ritard*

31

one of them is mine.

*a tempo*

*ritard* *pp*

CD 2 Track 38

# Loving You

Stephen Sondheim

Stephen Sondheim

**Largo tranquillo** ♩ = 56

*sempre legato*

*8va* *loco*

Lov-ing you is not a choice, It's who I am. ___

Lov - ing you is not a choice, And not much rea - son

Notes about this song are on page 299.

to re-joice, But it gives me pur-pose, Gives me voice to

*poco cresc.*

say to the world: _____ This is why I live.

*mp*

*dim.*

You are why I live. _____ Lov-ing you is

*p*

*mp*

why I do the things I do. _____

Lov-ing you is not in my con-trol._____ But lov-ing you, I have a goal, for what's left of my life._____ I will live, And I would die for you._____

# Whistle Down the Wind

Jim Steinman

Andrew Lloyd Webber

**Moderato con moto**

Whis-tle down the wind _____ Let your voic-es car - ry _____

Drown out all the rain   Light a patch of dark-ness treach-er-ous and sca - ry _____

Howl _ at the stars _____   Whis-per when you're sleep-ing _____

Notes about this song are on page 299.

# A | Notes on the Songs

Songs tell stories, but they also have their own stories. Here you can learn more about them and about the poets and composers who created the songs. Some songs come from plays, musicals, or operas that you want to know about, and it is helpful to know what instruments originally played the music.

A question may arise about singing in foreign languages. Your highest priority now is to improve your vocal sound and technique. If singing in another language makes it hard for you to sing well, it is better to sing an English translation or a different song. But if you have some background or a strong desire to sing in another language, it can add to your fun.

You first need to understand the text completely, whatever language it is. Translations are helpful if you understand the three kinds that exist:

1. *Singable* translations, in which the meaning is always somewhat different from the original because of the need for rhythm and rhyme

2. *Literal* translations with normal English word order, given in this book at the foot of the music pages, and

3. *Word-by-word* translations, such as are given on the following pages, showing exactly what each word means even when the word order makes the English sound unnatural.

Your next need is to pronounce the words correctly. Here you will find IPA transcriptions to help you, as well as general comments about some languages. Please understand that this book is not large enough to tell everything about any language. Just the essential information is given, so that if you have some background in the language and assistance from your teacher, you can sing the song correctly and confidently.

Foreign-language songs offered here are in Italian (four songs), Spanish (four), French, German, Hebrew, Japanese, Latin, and Swedish.

These languages differ in the number of vowels used, but all of them have pure vowels, that is, no vowels with diphthong shadings such as English has in "so" and "say." Give every vowel a constant quality for as long as it lasts.

Except for French and Japanese, all of these languages have stronger (stressed) and weaker (unstressed) syllables. Transcriptions in this book indicate stress by underlining.

**Songs for group singing**

"**America the Beautiful,**" page 94, was inspired by the view from Pike's Peak. Katherine Lee Bates, professor of English at Wellesley College, wrote the words on the morning after climbing Pike's Peak during a Colorado vacation in 1893. The tune by Samuel A. Ward is somewhat older, dating from 1882. The tune and words were published together in 1910.

"**Auld Lang Syne,**" page 94, means "old long since" and refers to times past. It has become an international tradition to sing it on New Year's Eve. While an early version of the poem has been traced to Sir Robert Ayton (1570–1638), we now know the words as Robert Burns wrote them down in 1791 from the singing of an old man. The tune may not be Scottish at all; it was claimed as an original composition by William Shield (1748–1829), who used it in 1783 in the overture to his opera *Rosina*.

The message of the song: "Should we forget old friendships? No, let's drink to them." "A cup of kindness" = a friendly drink; "gie's a hand of thine" = give me your hand.

"**Come, Follow!**" page 95, comes from *Catch That Catch Can* (1652). What we now call rounds were then called "catches."

## Singing in Spanish

Spanish is more legato than English, and the end of a word connects smoothly to the beginning of the next word.

Vowels carry the expressive message, just as in Italian. Spanish has many dialects, all using the same five vowel sounds. Spanish [i, o, u] are all pronounced a little more open than in Italian. Spanish [e] is much more open than Italian [e].

For the most part Spanish consonants are even softer than Italian consonants. There is no burst of air (aspiration) on plosive consonants [p, k, t]. The letters B, C, D, G, S, V, and Z all vary in pronunciation according to their locations. The sounds [d, t] are dental sounds, pronounced with the tongue tip touching the teeth.

R may be either flipped [ɾ] or rolled [r]. LL is [j] in Latin American texts, but [ʎ] in songs from Spain.

IPA symbols are listed in Appendix B.

"**De colores,**" page 95, a happy song about Nature, is universally known and loved in Mexico.

IPA    de    kolores se              βisten los kampos en la    primaβera
       De    colores se              visten los campos en la    primavera,
       With colors   themselves dress   the fields    in the spring,

       son los paxarijos   ke   βjenen de   fwera
... son los pajarillos   que   vienen de   fuera,
       are the little-birds that come   from far-away,

       es el   arkoiris   ke   βemos lusir
... es el   arcoiris   que vemos lucir,
       is the rainbow that we-see shining,

i      por eso los grandes amores de mutʃos kolores
Y      por eso los grandes amores de muchos colores
and for this the great    loves   of many    colors

me ɣustan   a mi
Me gustan   a mí.
are pleasing to me.

"**Do-Re-Mi,**" page 96. Set in Austria in 1937–38, *The Sound of Music* is based on the true story of Maria Rainer, the young governess of seven children. She married their father and became Baroness Maria von Trapp. When the family escaped Nazi persecution by emigrating, she led the children into an international concert career as the Trapp Family Singers. Mary Martin proposed putting their story on stage, and she created the leading role.

**"Greeting Song,"** page 96, was taught to me by Dr. William (Komla) Omoaku, Director of the National Theater of Ghana. Move while singing it (two steps right, two steps left) and clap on beats 2 and 4.

**"He's Got the Whole World in His Hands,"** page 97, was first published in Edward Boatner's *Spirituals Triumphant* (Nashville, 1927). The melody is given here as Marian Anderson sang it on a 1962 recording. Anderson, who was the greatest concert singer of her time and the first black artist ever to sing at the Metropolitan Opera, sang this spiritual at the rally in Washington, D.C., where Dr. Martin Luther King Jr. delivered his historic "I Have a Dream" speech.

**"Hinay Ma Tov,"** page 97, is a popular Israeli melody. Sing each line twice. To sing this as a two-part round, the second group enters when the first group begins the second line. Repeat as many times as you like, both parts sounding together. The "ch" sound is pronounced [x], as in German *"Bach."*

IPA: hinei ma tov uma nayim
Hinay ma tov uma nayim
Behold what-is good and-is pleasant:

ʃɛvɛt axim gam jaxad
shevet achim gam yachad.
to-remain brothers also together.

**"Let There Be Peace on Earth,"** page 98. Beginning in m. 16, the original words were "With God as our Father, Brothers all are we; let me walk with my brother . . ."

**"Scarborough Fair,"** page 99, is a humorous song about a former sweetheart. You promise to be sweethearts again in return for three tasks that, in fact, are quite impossible.

The tune was made famous by Paul Simon and Art Garfunkel in the movie *The Graduate,* but many other versions also exist. The words given here were sung in 1891 by a fisherman from North Riding, Yorkshire. Mr. Moat sang two complete texts, one for a woman and one for a man. Each ends with this stanza:

And now I have answered your questions three,
I hope you'll answer as many for me.
I hope you'll answer as many for me,
 And then thou shalt be a true lover of mine.

Of course, there are no answers to the impossible challenges. These words and the melodies Mr. Moat sang are found in *English Country Songs* by Lucy E. Broadwood and J. A. Fuller Maitland (London: Leadenhall Press, 1893).

**"Sing and Rejoice!"** page 99, was taught to me by my late friend, Prof. Arthur Becknell. The source is unknown.

**"The Star-Spangled Banner,"** page 100. Francis Scott Key, district attorney for Washington, D.C., was on board a ship in Baltimore harbor, unable to land during the nighttime bombardment of Fort McHenry by the British in 1814. When morning light revealed that the fort had not surrendered, Key wrote this poem, expressing his pride. The tune is an English drinking song of the 1700s, "To Anacreon in Heaven." The United States had no official anthem until 1931, when this song was chosen. Lower notes (not part of the official anthem) are suggested here for those who are uncomfortable with the wide range of the song.

**"This Little Light of Mine,"** page 101, has a Biblical basis in Matthew 5:16: "Let your light so shine before men that they may see your good works and glorify your Father . . ." The tune is sung many ways: if you know another version, sing it. Swing the rhythms.

**"Viva la musica!"** page 101. Michael Praetorius (German, 1571–1621) also wrote the Christmas song "Lo, How a Rose E'er Blooming."

# Traditional songs

"All the Notes of All the Earth," page 102, uses a minor scale with alterations that are typical of Roma (gypsy) music. It was published with English words only in *Folk-Songs of Eastern Europe,* edited by Ralph Radcliffe Whitehead (Boston: Oliver Ditson, 1912).

"Auprès de ma blonde," page 104, a lively song from Normandy in northern France, celebrates the love of a happy young wife and husband. Notice that the bride's three verses all form one long sentence, interrupted by the man's refrain. This alternation means that anyone can sing this song, making it widely popular.

IPA      o       ʒar dẽ  də mõ  pɛ rə
1. Au      jardin  de mon père
   At-the garden of  my  father

le  lɔr je   sõ  flœ ri
Les lauriers sont fleuri,
the laurels  are  flowered;

tu  le zwa zo dy    mõ də
Tous les oiseaux du     monde
all  the birds   of-the world

võ  ti   fɛ rə    lœr ni
Vont y    faire    leur nids . . .
go   there to-make their nests . . .

          o prɛ   də ma blõ də
Refrain:  Auprès de ma blonde
          Close   to  my blonde (wife)

kil  fɛ   bõ  dɔr mir
Qu'il fait bon dormir!
how-it does good to-sleep!

     la  kaj   la  tur tə rɛ lə
2. La  caill', la  tourterelle
   The quail, the turtledove

e   lə  ʒɔ li   pɛr dri
Et  le  joli    partridge
and the pretty partridge

e   la  blã ʃə   kɔ lõ bə
Et  la  blanche colombe
and the white    dove,

ki  ʃã tə  ʒu  re nɥi
Qui chante jour et  nuit . . .
who sings  day and night . . .

     ɛl  ʃã tə  pur lɛ  fi jə
3. Elle chante pour les  filles
   She sings  for   the girls

ki  nõ      pwẽ də ma ri
Qui n'ont    point de mari;
who not-have any  of husband;

sɛ   pɑ pur mwa kɛl     ʃã tə
C'est pas pour moi qu'ell'  chante,
it-is not for   me   that-she sings,

kar   ʒã  ne   œ̃ ʒɔ li
Car   j'en ai   un joli.
because I-one have, a  handsome-one.

**"Carmela,"** page 106, seems to be a Mexican popular song of the 1800s. It was written down by Eleanor Hague and arranged by Gertrude Ross in *Early Spanish-Californian Folk-Songs* (New York: J. Fischer & Bro., 1922).

IPA: asi kwal mweren en oksiðente los tiβjos rajos del   astro rei
Así cual  mueren en occidente los tibios rayos del   astro rey,
Just as  die   in west      the weak rays of-the star  king,

asi murjeron mis ilusjones asi ekstingjendose va   mi fe.
Así murieron mis ilusiones, así extinguiéndose va   mi fe.
so  will-die  my dreams,  so dying-away     goes my faith.

karmen karmela lus ðe mis oxos
Carmen, Carmela, luz  de mis ojos,
Carmen, Carmen, light of my  eyes,

si lus  no uβjera aβias          ðe ser
Si luz  no hubiera, habías        de ser.
if light not I-had,   you-would-have to be (my light).

ermoso faro   ðe βenturansa
Hermoso faro   de venturanza,
lovely    beacon of good-fortune,

duls esperansa beʎo    plaser
Dulce esperanza, bello    placer.
sweet hope,      beautiful pleasure.

perla presjosa ðe mis amores ke   son las flores  xunto a ti
Perla preciosa de mis amores, que   son las flores  junto a ti?
Pearl precious of  my love,    what are the flowers next to you?

ʤo las kontemplo una por una i   noai   ninguna iɣal a ti
Yo las  contemplo una por una, y   no hay ninguna igual a ti.
I  them consider  one by one,  and not have any     equal to you.

**"Cielito lindo,"** page 108, is one of the most popular songs to come out of Mexico. Published versions go back to the 1920s, but the song is certainly much older.

IPA  de   la sjera      morena βjenen baxando
De    la Sierra       Morena vienen bajando
From the Mountains Brown    come   descending

un par deoxitos    neɣros sjelito      lindo ðe kontraβando
Un par de ojitos    negros, cielito      lindo, de contrabando.
a   pair of dear-eyes dark,    dear-Heaven lovely, of contraband.

ai kanta i   no jores
Ay, canta y   no llores,
Ah, sing  and not weep,

porke  kantando se aleɣran    los korasones
Porque cantando se alegran    los corazones.
because singing –   are-happy, the hearts.

paxaro keaβandona   su primer niðo
Pajaro que abandona su primer nido
Bird    that leaves    its first   nest

reɣresa i  ja no      enkwentra    el βjen  perðiðo
Regresa y  ya no      encuentra    el bien  perdido.
returns and now doesn't meet        the darling lost.

ese lunar ke tjenes    xuntoa la βoka
Ese lunar que tienes . . . junto a la  boca
That mole that you-have, next  to the mouth,

no        se lo ðes  a  na̯ðje     kea   mi me t̯oka
No       se lo des  a  nadie . . . que a mí me toca.
don't –   it  give to anyone   because [idiom: it's mine].

**"Deep River,"** page 112, appears in the oldest collections of Negro spirituals, published a few years after the Civil War. Spirituals are the songs that the slaves developed to keep up their spirits and express their longing for a better life. Here, the Jordan River symbolizes going to that better place, either in death or in liberation. This version was arranged by Henry Thacker Burleigh (1866–1949), a black baritone and composer. When he studied in New York City, Antonin Dvořák was there as a guest professor. Dvořák befriended Burleigh and learned about American music by listening to him sing spirituals. After long neglect, Burleigh's serious compositions are again receiving concert performances.

I do not recommend singing black dialect unless it comes naturally to you, but consonants should be sung gently.

**"Down by the Salley Gardens,"** page 116, has a poem by the eminent Irish poet William Butler Yeats (1865–1939). The poem was matched to an old tune, "The Maids of Mourne Shore," by Herbert Hughes. "Salley" is derived from a Gaelic word for "willow." It was once common to raise gardens of willows to provide materials for basket making and thatched roofs. "Weirs" = dams or embankments to divert water.

Source: *Irish Country Songs* (London, 1909).

**"Drink to Me Only with Thine Eyes,"** page 120, has a poem by Ben Jonson (1572–1637), an actor and writer only eight years younger than Shakespeare. The anonymous melody is English, from the 1700s. "Jove" = king of the Roman gods; "nectar" = the gods' preferred drink; "change" = trade. The richly pianistic accompaniment was written by Roger Quilter and dedicated to the memory of Arnold Guy Vivian.

Source: *The Arnold Book of Old Songs* (London: Boosey and Hawkes, 1921).

**"Love Will Find Out the Way,"** page 125. The tune, first published in 1652 in Playford's *Musick's Recreation*, was still current in England as a folk song in the 1800s. The words were published in 1765 in Percy's *Reliques of Ancient English Poetry*.

**"Sakura, Sakura,"** page 128, was first published in Japan in 1883. In Puccini's opera *Madama Butterfly* (1904), the orchestra plays the melody as Butterfly reveals the few possessions she has brought with her into marriage. The piano accompaniment, written especially for this book, uses the same scale as the melody, a traditional Japanese scale called "Rissenpoh" with five notes: mi, fa, la, ti, do. Thanks to Prof. Yasushi Shiba for this information and to Takaaki Hara for the following word-by-word translation.

Sakura,                sakura,          Yayoi  no sorawa,
Cherry-blossoms, cherry-blossoms, March, its  sky,

Miwatasu      kagiri,  Kasumi ka kumoka
look-around insofar, mist      or  cloud,

Nioizo         izuru,   Izaya, izaya miniyukan
fragrance-is coming, let's   let's  to-see-go.

Pronunciation of Japanese: The vowels are as in Spanish, except U, which is [y], as in French "lune" or German "kühn." The last note of the song is sung on [ŋ] with no vowel.

**"The Turtle Dove,"** page 130, is one of many English folk songs named after this gentle bird. Ralph Vaughan Williams arranged this melody for baritone solo and chorus (1924).

# Art songs and arias
## The Renaissance period

Most of the artistic music composed during the Renaissance was choral music for church use. At the very end of the Renaissance, in Elizabethan England, new techniques in music printing and a new level of prosperity led to a flood of new songs for voice and lute. No other period has known so many good composers who wrote both poetry and music.

"**It Was a Lover and His Lass,**" page 132, may have been written especially for a Shakespearean play. Thomas Morley (1557–1602) and Shakespeare (1564–1616) were neighbors for a time in London and were undoubtedly acquainted. Morley was organist at St. Paul's Cathedral and a musician at the court of Elizabeth I.

The song occurs near the end of *As You Like It*, sung by two page boys for the amusement of a clown and his bride-to-be. The scene contains some clever comments on amateur singing. "Cornfield" = wheat field, "ringtime" = wedding season.

Performance: Imagine the bridal couple dancing and keep the tempo moving. In the changing meters at m. 25 and m. 26, keep the quarter notes moving evenly and put stresses where the words require them. Elizabethan composers often used such tricks to keep their rhythms lively.

Accompaniment: Morley asked for lute and bass viol; guitar and cello would be next best. Symbols for the lute show exactly what notes to play, including the interesting chromatic changes. This edition gives voice and bass parts exactly as Morley wrote them; harmonies are adapted so that the pianist doubles the singer's notes.

Source: *First Booke of Ayres* (London, 1600), reproduced in facsimile in *English Lute Songs*, vol. 8, no. 33. Meter: Alla breve. Key: G major with no signature. Voice part in G clef, beginning on g1. Shakespeare's poem has four stanzas.

"**Since First I Saw Your Face,**" page 138. Thomas Ford (15??–1648) was a musician at the royal court in London.

Accompaniment: The voice and bass parts given here are authentic, but the harmonization is adapted to the piano from the original for lute.

Source: *Musick of Sundrie Kindes* (London, 1607). Key: C. The lute tablature is also reproduced in *Ten Airs*, edited by Fellowes and Dart (London: Stainer & Bell, 1966).

"**The Silver Swan,**" page 142, is based on a myth that swans lose their ugly cry and sing beautifully once just before dying. This idea carries a feeling that one's best times are past, that the future has no joy in store. Orlando Gibbons (1583–1625), organist at the Chapel Royal in London, came to the court of James I after Morley died, but he must have known Ford.

This song is arranged from a madrigal that was "apt for Viols and Voyces." It could be performed by five voices or by one voice accompanied by four viols (stringed instruments).

Source: *First Set of Madrigals and Motets* (London, 1612). Key: F.

## The Baroque period

The English songs described above used a Renaissance style that was coming to a close at the same time a new musical style, the Baroque, was being born in Italy. It grew out of the dramatic needs of opera, a newly invented performing art, in which a poetic play is sung throughout. Usually recognized as the first opera was *Euridice* by Jacopo Peri, performed in Florence, Italy, in 1600 on the occasion of a royal wedding.

The new feature of opera was an accompaniment with slow chords over which the singer had the utmost freedom to sing words expressively, not being bound to a steady rhythm. Single notes in the bass part indicated the chords, which were filled in by players who improvised on keyboard or fretted instruments. Because the bass was constantly present, we call it the *basso continuo*. The interaction of the melody and bass became the identifying mark of Baroque style.

## Singing in Italian

The classical technique of singing comes from Italy. Many teachers prefer to have students sing in Italian before any other language. The typical Italian sound is *legato* (tied), or smooth. The end of a word is nearly always connected smoothly to the beginning of the next word. The flow of connected sounds is broken only by certain double consonants.

Italian vowels, not consonants, convey the energy and emotion of the language. Every stressed vowel followed by a single consonant is lengthened, as in *cane* [kaːne].

Italian spelling often resembles IPA symbols, with some exceptions. The letters *e* and *o* each have two pronunciations in stressed syllables, closed and open, and the spelling does not indicate which one to use. Every *e* or *o* in a stressed syllable must be checked with a dictionary. (In unstressed syllables they are always closed.)

Consonants are gentle in Italian. [p, t, k] have no aspiration (explosiveness). [d, n, t, l] are all pronounced with the tongue lightly touching the upper teeth (dentalized).

Italian double consonants are audibly different from single ones. If possible, the consonant sound continues for at least three times as long as it takes to say a single consonant, shown in IPA this way [mːm sːs bːb]. When the doubled consonant is a voiceless stop, there is silence between the closing and reopening of the consonant, for example, *attacca* [atːakːka]. This is an exception to the legato rule.

*R* is pronounced with a single flip of the tongue-tip [ɾ] when it occurs between two vowels; otherwise it is vigorously rolled [r].

IPA symbols are listed in Appendix B.

**"Dolce scherza,"** page 146. Giacomo Antonio Perti (1661–1754) was a prominent composer and teacher in Bologna, Italy.

Accompaniment: The composer expected a harpsichord and cello to play from the same bass part, with the harpsichordist improvising chords. Here the chords have been filled in by the editor; feel free to change them as you like. Use no pedal; let the chords be detached when appropriate.

Source: No primary source is available. A romanticized version of this aria appeared in *Bel Canto* (Braunschweig, c1900) by Albert Fuchs, who found it in the State Library of Dresden, Germany. The original was stolen during World War II but may still exist in Russia. Using Fuchs's version, I have tried to guess what the original may be like.

IPA  doltʃe   skertsa e   doltʃe   riːde
     Dolce    scherza e   dolce    ride
     Sweetly jests    and sweetly laughs

     vaːgo  labːbro e   spiːra   amoːr
     Vago   labbro e    spira    amor.
     lovely lip      and breathes love.

     ma talːletːta   e   poi tutːtʃiːde
     Ma t'alletta        e   poi t'uccide;
     But you-it-cheers and then you-kills;

     kozi afːfliddʒe kwesto kɔr
     Così affligge   questo cor.
     thus it-harms this     heart

**"Io le dirò che l'amo,"** page 150, comes from an opera composed in 1738, *Serse*, by George Frideric Handel (1685–1759). Born in Germany, Handel lived for three years in Italy and earned a reputation as a leading opera composer. Refusing employment offers on the Continent, he settled in London, which then offered more personal and political freedom than anywhere else in the world.

A song from an opera is usually called an *aria* (Italian for "air"). An aria occurs when a situation in the story produces an emotion that the character needs to express. In Baroque operas the conversations between characters were sung in *recitative*, a style in which the music has very little melodic interest because it follows the inflection of the words and is accompanied only by a keyboard instrument and a cello. Arias have strong melodies, repetition of important words, and usually orchestral accompaniment.

This aria is sung by the title character, known as Serse in Italian or as Xerxes in English. The historical Xerxes (519–465 B.C.E.) was a king of Persia. The operatic Xerxes bears little resemblance to him. Stories of ancient kings were of interest to Baroque audiences because they explored issues that could not be so openly discussed as they are now: How should a ruler behave? What is justice? How should one resolve conflicting duties?

The situation here is that Serse has asked his brother to deliver a message of love to a certain lady. Serse's brother, being secretly in love with the same lady, produces various excuses to avoid the errand. Serse decides in this aria to approach the lady himself and declare his love.

At the end of m. 19, you are instructed to go back to the beginning and start over *da capo*, "from the top." *Da capo arias* were popular with audiences because they meant that a good tune could be enjoyed twice. Also, repetition allowed the singer to add ornaments to the melody, in somewhat the same way as a jazz player improvises on a popular song. A quick tune like this one does not need many ornaments, but feel free to make up your own.

Handel's opera company employed some of Italy's most famous singers, and this aria was written for Caffarelli, a male soprano whose name is still part of the history of opera. Most of his arias were technically difficult show pieces; this one, being relatively simple, emphasizes sensitive feeling.

Accompaniment: Full-sized notes indicate the original orchestration as far as possible. Smaller notes fill in harmonies as they might have been played by the keyboard player, whose part was not written out by the composer.

Source: *Werke*, vol. 92. For voice (soprano clef), two violins, viola and continuo. Key: G.

IPA: io le dirɔ    ke laːmo
Io le dirò      che l'amo,
I   her will-say that her-I-love,

ne mi zgomenterɔ
né mi sgomenterò.
nor – shall-I-be-alarmed.

e    perke  mia la braːmo
E    perché mia la bramo,
And because mine her I-desire

sɔ   kwel ke    far  dovrɔ
So   quel che    far  dovrò.
I-know that which to-do I-ought.

The aria could be sung in English with the following translation: "I will say I love her, Nor will I be afraid, For if I want to win her, I know what I must do!"

**The Classical period**

As the Classical style developed in the works of J. S. Bach's sons and the works of Haydn, the piano became many composers' favorite instrument because it was stronger and more expressive than the harpsichord. Musicians gave up the

Baroque custom of improvising keyboard accompaniments over a *basso continuo* and used fully written out accompaniments, both for keyboard and for orchestra.

**"Sigh No More, Ladies,"** page 154, comes from Shakespeare's *Much Ado About Nothing*, Act II:3. Richard John Samuel Stevens (1757–1837) composed it as a *glee*, a song for several voices, but it has been sung as a solo in many productions of the play.

Source: *Songs of England*, edited by J. L. Hatton and Eaton Faning (London, no date). Key: A.

**"Bitten,"** page 160, shows how simply one of the greatest composers of all time could write. Ludwig van Beethoven (1770–1827) composed it in 1803, the same year as his Symphony No. 3, the magnificent "Eroica."

Beethoven probably meant his *Six Songs of Gellert* to be sung at home. German sacred songs were not used in the Roman Catholic churches of Austria, and there were still not many public concerts that featured songs. The poems, written by Christian Fuerchtegott Gellert (1715–69), were widely known and had been set to music earlier by C. P. E. Bach, one of the musical sons of the great J. S. Bach.

Performance: Beethoven loved singers and singing, but he demanded the utmost of all performers. Even this brief song has one strenuous passage, mm. 27–32, where the voice stays on one pitch in the upper part of the voice. Be sure to breathe often enough, even at every comma, to stay physically free. Notice that m. 33 is suddenly soft after a long crescendo; Beethoven liked this effect and used it also in m. 15 and m. 36.

Accompaniment: Notice how often Beethoven used slurs in the left hand, indicating that the bass should sound melodic and interesting.

Source: *Sechs Lieder von Gellert*, Opus 48, no. 1 (1803). Key: E. Tempo marking: "Feierlich und mit Andacht."

"Bitten," Ludwig van Beethoven
[bɪtːtən luːtvɪc fan beːthoːfən]

IPA  gɔt dᶏenə gyːtə    raeçt  zoː vaet
Gott, deine Güte    reicht  so  weit,
God, your  goodness reaches as  far

zo vaet diː vᵓlkən geːən
So weit die Wolken gehen,
as far  the clouds go.

duː krøːnst ʊns mɪt  barmhᵉrtsɪçkaet
Du krönst uns mit Barmherzigkeit,
You crown  us  with compassion

ʊnt aelst ʊns bᶏetsuːʃteːən
Und eilst  uns beizustehen.
and hurry us  by-to-stand.

hɛr  mᶏenə bʊrk    mᶏen fɛls  mᶏen hɔrt
Herr, meine Burg,    mein Fels, mein Hort
Lord, my  fortress, my   rock, my    protection,

fɛrnɪm   maen fleːn    mɛrk |aof maen vɔrt
Vernimm mein Flehn,    merk' auf mein Wort,
Hear     my  pleading, notice –  my    word,

dɛn ɪç vɪl foːr  diːr beːtən
Denn ich will vor    dir beten!
for  I  want before you to-pray.

## The Romantic period

The 1800s, beginning with the tumult of the Napoleonic Wars, brought radical changes into Western people's lives. The breakdown of old monarchies led to rebelliousness among students and intellectuals. Individual freedoms took on new importance, and individual emotions became the focus of a new artistic movement, Romanticism. There was great poverty (think of Dickens's *A Christmas Carol*) and pervasive social injustice. At the same time, industrialization produced a growing middle class. A piano in the family's parlor was an acknowledged symbol of financial stability.

**"Who Is Sylvia?"** page 164, combines words by the greatest English poet with music by the greatest German song composer. Franz Schubert (1797–1828) learned the Classical style from singing as a boy soprano in the choir of the Imperial Chapel and from composition lessons with Antonio Salieri (Mozart's nemesis in the movie and play *Amadeus*). Poetry led him to Romanticism, and he admired Shakespeare, as other Romantics did. Often supported by friends, he lived in poverty and died at age 31.

The text was translated into German from Shakespeare's *Two Gentlemen of Verona*, Act 4, scene 2. One of the gentlemen, Proteus, has arranged a serenade in honor of Sylvia, the daughter of the Duke of Milan. Proteus has written the words of the song, and it is sung either by him or by one of the hired musicians.

Schubert's works are known by catalog numbers given to them by O. E. Deutsch. This song is D. 891, meaning that it is estimated to be Schubert's 891st composition.

While you sing, listen to the melodic bass part in the pianist's left hand; think of your melody as a graceful counterpart to the bouncing bass melody.

"What is she?" = what is her nature?; "swains" = young men; "kind" = generous to a lover; "repair" = pay a visit; "excels" = is better than. Love, in the person of Cupid, is said to be blind, but he is no longer blind if he lives in Sylvia's eyes.

Source: *An Sylvia*, D. 891 (July 1826). Key: A. Tempo: *Mässig*.

**"Beautiful Dreamer,"** page 169, is a masterwork of a minor artist, Stephen Collins Foster (Pittsburgh, 1826–New York City, 1864). His earlier songs, written for minstrel shows, are marred by racial stereotypes; but later Foster abandoned black dialect and broadened his subject matter. His 200 songs have been published in many kinds of arrangements, none of which are as clear, tasteful, and correct as Foster's original versions.

Source: *Beautiful Dreamer; Serenade* (New York: W. A. Pond, 1864, first edition). Key: E♭.

**"Santa Lucia,"** page 172, universally known as an Italian folksong, was written in 1850 by Teodoro Cottrau (1827–79), a music publisher in Naples. The waterfront of old Naples lies within the parish of the church of St. Lucia. Here, a sailor invites us to ride to Naples in his boat.

Source: *Songs of Italy* (London: before 1900?). Key: D-flat.

IPA   sul      maːre lutːtʃika lastro dardʒɛnto
      Sul      mare luccica l'astro d'argento,
      On-the-sea   shines   the-star of-silver;

      plaːtʃidaɛ londa prɔsperoɛil vɛnto
      Placida  è l'onda, prospero  è il  vento.
      calm    is the-sea, favorable  is the wind.

      venite alːlaːdʒile     barkɛtːta mia santa lutʃia
      Venite all'agile     barchetta mia! Santa Lucia!
      Come to-the-graceful little-boat mine! St. Lucia!

      kon  kwɛsto dʒɛfːfiro kozi soaːve
      Con  questo zeffiro  così soave,
      With this    breeze  so  gentle,

oː koːmɛ  bɛlːlo   staːr sulːla naːve
O com'è   bello   star sulla nave!
O how-it-is beautiful to-be on-the ship!

suː pasːsadːʤɛri veniͭte viͣa
Su passaggieri,  venite via!   Santa Lucia!
Up, passengers!  come away!

**"Willow, Tit-Willow,"** page 176, comes from *The Mikado*, an operetta (musical play) that pretends to be about life in Japan. In fact, it lampoons English social customs, as do all the operettas written by William S. Gilbert and Sir Arthur Sullivan (1842–1900).

This tale of mock tragedy can be sung by anyone, but in the operetta it is sung by Ko-Ko, an executioner. For complicated reasons, he needs to persuade Katisha, an unattractive older woman, that he will kill himself if she refuses his love. She accepts him, and like all operettas, this one has a happy ending.

Source: *The Mikado* (London, 1885).

**"In Haven,"** page 180, paints a picture of contented lovers on a seashore where the waves lap gently. The subtitle, "Capri," refers to the scenic island in the Mediterranean near Naples. The poem is by Carol Alice Elgar, the wife of the composer. Edward Elgar (1857–1934) was the most successful English composer of his time, and his symphonic works are still performed often.

Source: *Sea Pictures*, Opus 37 (London, 1899).

**"E l'uccellino,"** page 184. The great opera composer Giacomo Puccini (1858–1924) composed this charming lullaby for the infant son of one of his best friends, who had died before the baby was born. It has been a successful recital piece, recorded by major artists like Licia Albanese and Renata Tebaldi, and it can also be sung appropriately by male singers.

Source: first edition (Milan, 1899). Key: D.

IPA  e   lutːtʃelːliͭno  kaͣnta sulːla froͭnda
     E   l'uccellino    canta sulla fronda:
     And the-little-bird sings on-the leafy-branch:

doͭrmi traŋkwiͭlːlo bokːkutːtʃa damoːre
Dormi tranquillo, boccuccia  d'amore;
sleep peacefully, dear-mouth of-love;

pjɛːgala ʤu  kwɛlːla testiːͭna  bjoͭnda
Piegala giù,  quella testina   bionda,
bend-it down, that  little-head fair,

delːla tuͣa  maͣmːma poͭːzala sul  kwoͭːre
Della tua   mamma posala sul   cuore.
of   your mama,  put-it on-the heart.
(put your head on your mama's heart.)

               kaͣnta su kwɛl raːmo
     E   l'uccellino   canta su quel ramo,
     And the-little-bird sings on that branch;

taͣnte  koziːͭne  bɛlːle  impareraͣi
Tante  cosine   belle   imparerai,
so-many dear-things beautiful you-will-learn,

ma se vorːraͣi  konoʃːʃer kwantiːͭo  taːmo
Ma se vorrai   conoscer quant'io   t'amo,
but if you-want to-know  how-much-I you-love,

nesːsuͭːno al moͭndo potraͣ diͭrlo maͣi
Nessuno al mondo potrà dirlo mai!
no-one   on earth   could say-it ever!

                kᴀntal      ʧɛl sereːno
E   l'uccellino   canta al   ciel sereno:
And the-little-bird sings to-the sky  peaceful:

dᴏrmi tezᴏːro mi̯o  kwi sul mi̯o seːno
Dormi tesoro  mio  qui sul mio seno.
sleep,  treasure mine, here on  my  bosom.

## The twentieth century

Around 1900 many musicians believed that composers like Wagner and Richard Strauss had stretched conventional ways of composing to the breaking point and that completely new ways had to be found. Charles Ives was one of the searchers, but he worked alone, unknown to other musicians. Igor Stravinsky, Paul Hindemith, and Béla Bartók were among the international musicians who found new paths and influenced music in the twentieth century.

    **"Star-Eyes,"** page 190, is a melancholy recollection of someone whom the poet loved for years but never married. Wilhelm Stenhammar (1871–1927) said that a song should have "a simple melody that hugs the sound of the words." One of Sweden's most eminent musicians, Stenhammar composed many large works and 67 songs. Thanks to Sten Neiker of Arvika, Sweden, for introducing me to this song, for the word-by-word translation, and for the IPA.

    Source: *Five Songs by Bo Bergman*, Opus 20 (1903–4).

IPA  ʃæːrnøːga dʉː  sᴏm jɑːg møt
      Stjärnöga, du  som jag  mött
      Star-eye,  you that I     met

      loːŋt    iː fœrsvᴏna tiːdɛr
      Långt   i  försvunna tider,
      far-away in vanished   times,

      nʉː æːr dɛ kvɛldaks ᴏ  trøt
      Nu  är  det kvälldags, och trött
      now is   it  night-time, and tired,

      mɪn ᴏŋdʉm tɪl viːla skriːdɛr
      min ungdom till vila skrider.
      my youth    to  rest proceeds.

      ɪrblᴏs          sᴏm væːrdɛn hɑːr tɛnt
      Irrbloss,      som  världen har tänt,
      Will-o'-the-wisp, which world  has  lit,

      slᴏkna   soː lɛt    iː væːrdɛn
      Slockna  så lätt   i  världen.
      goes-out so  easily in world.

      ʃæːrnøːga mɣkət hɑːr hɛnt
      Stjärnöga, mycket har hänt,
      Star-eye,   much  has  happened

      seːdan viː ʃɪldɛs poː fæːrdɛn
      Sedan vi  skildes på  färden.
      since  we parted on  the-way.

      vɪlsam    ær vɛːgɛn sᴏm   goːr
      Vilsam    är vägen som   går
      Confusing is  road   which passes

      fram jeːnᴏm mœrka lɛndɛr
      Fram genom mörka länder.
      ahead through dark    countries.

ʃæːrnøːga ʃæːrnøːga noːr
Stjärnöga, Stjärnöga, når
Star-Eye,              reach

jɑːg ɑldrig meːr diːna hɛndɛr
Jag  aldrig mer  dina  händer?
I    never  again your hands?

tɑːg miːna hɛndɛr ɔ  leːd
Tag  mina  händer och led
Take my   hands  and lead

miːg ɪn iː dɪt  jʉːsa rɨːkɛ
Mig  in i  ditt ljusa rike.
me   in to your light empire.

ʃæːrnøːga jiːv miːg dɪn freːd
Stjärnöga, giv mig din  fred
Star-Eye,  give me  your peace

ɔ  loːt miːg vɑːrda dɪn liːkɛ
Och låt mig varda  din like.
and let me  become your equal.

**"The Sky above the Roof,"** page 187. Ralph Vaughan Williams (1872–1958) based his style on scales and rhythms found in English folk songs. The poem is translated from *"Le ciel est, par-dessus le toit,"* written by Paul Verlaine (1844–96) while he was in prison for attempted murder.

**"Serenity,"** page 194, has only a few notes, but it is challenging to control the rhythms in a slow tempo. Charles Edward Ives (Danbury, CT, 1874–New York City, 1954) studied music at Yale but made a fortune in the life insurance field. Encouraged by his wife, Harmony, Ives wrote music in his leisure hours. He made remarkable musical innovations, including use of several keys at once and novel ways of forming chords. His stressful life led to a heart attack in 1918. During his recuperation Ives "cleaned house" by making final copies of music written earlier, including this song, finished in 1919. He lived to see a growing acceptance of his music, which is now played often by major symphony orchestras.

This text comes near the end of "The Brewing of Soma" by John Greenleaf Whittier (1872), which is a plea for a simple and direct access to divine truth. The last stanzas of the poem, including this text, are sung as a hymn that begins "Dear Lord and Father of Mankind." Ives often quoted from well-known hymns.

Source: *114 Songs* (printed privately at Ives's expense, 1922).

**"Serenade,"** page 196. Gena Branscombe (Picton, Ontario, 1881–New York, 1977) studied at the Chicago Musical College, and she was teaching there when she published this song (1905). She later conducted the Branscombe Chorale for 22 years and published more than 150 songs and 60 choral pieces. The text, excerpted from *In a Gondola*, reflects the atmosphere of Venice, where Robert Browning (1812–89) lived his last years.

**"By the Sea,"** page 198. Roger Quilter (1877–1953) wrote both words and music of this song when he was in his early twenties.

Source: *Three Songs of the Sea* (London: Forsyth, 1911).

**"Fancy,"** page 201, is a unique work in English by a master of French song. In *The Merchant of Venice*, Act III:2, this poem is sung as a coded message from Portia to Bassanio not to judge value by appearances alone. "Fancy" = superficial attraction, as opposed to true love.

Francis Poulenc (1899–1963) was the greatest French song composer of the 1900s. This is his only work in English, written at the request of Benjamin Britten. Poulenc fancifully dedicated the song "To Miles and Flora," who were not real persons, but the children in Britten's opera *The Turn of the Screw*.

**"Vos me matásteis,"** page 204, is an original composition by Joaquin Rodrigo (Spanish, 1901–98). Rodrigo took the poem and some melodic ideas from a song by the Renaissance composer Juan Vasquez. The original, composed for three voices and published in 1551, can be studied in Vasquez' *Villancicos i canciones,* edited by Eleanor Russell (Madison: A-R Editions, 1995).

Source: second song in *Cuatro madrigales amatorios.* Original key: F♯ minor.

IPA  bos me matasteis niɲa    en kaβeʎo
     Vos me matásteis, niña    en cabello,
     You me murdered, little-one in hair-hanging-loose.

     bos me aβeis mwerto
     vos me habeis muerto.
     you me have   killed.

     riβeras ðe un río   bi    moθa βirxen
     Riberas de un rio,  vi    moza virgen,
     Banks of a  river, I-saw young virgin.

**"The Lord Has a Child,"** page 208, an expression of simple faith, comes from a complex and sophisticated poet, Langston Hughes (1862–1948), a leader of the Harlem Renaissance. The music, which is simple in texture but sophisticated in harmonic language, is by William Schuman (New York, 1910–New York, 1992), a Pulitzer Prize winner in composition.

**"To a Brown Girl, Dead,"** page 212, presents a poignant picture of Harlem life. We do not know how the girl died, only that her mother has sacrificed to make her pretty. Countee Cullen (1903–46) was a lyric poet, a leader of the Harlem Renaissance. The poem comes from his book *Color* (1925). Margaret Bonds (Chicago, 1913–Los Angeles, 1972) was a versatile musician and prolific composer who collaborated with Langston Hughes on stage productions.

**"A Song Without Words,"** page 216, is an original vocalise that has also been performed as an instrumental solo. It was inspired by the almost wordless singing of a Texas blues artist, Blind Willie Johnson, in a recording called "Dark Was the Night."

Charles S. Brown (born 1940, Marianna, Arkansas) studied voice and composition at the University of Michigan. A bass-baritone, Brown has sung internationally, including the historic production of George Gershwin's *Porgy and Bess* at the Metropolitan Opera. He teaches in New York City and continues to compose and publish songs and choral arrangements.

Source: *Anthology of Art Songs by Black American Composers,* edited by Willis C. Patterson (New York: Edward B. Marks, 1977).

**"Lo, How a Rose,"** page 218, is based on an anonymous German Christmas poem from the 1500s, "Es ist ein Ros' entsprungen," translated into English by Theodore Baker (1894). Hughes Huffman, Jr. (born Hickory, N.C., 1942) has degrees in voice from Wheaton College and Northern Illinois University. He is a church music director in West Covina, CA. "Rose" = the baby Jesus; "Jesse" = the father of David and an ancestor of Jesus.

This is the first publication of this song, written in 1998.

IPA  ɔdiɛ   kristus  natus ɛst noɛl
     Hodie  Christus natus est. Noel.
     Today  Christ   born is.   Christmas.

## Musical theater songs and popular song classics

When a Broadway musical is developed, it usually goes through a long process in which songs are written and tried out, some of them re-written or discarded. Songs may be added, revised or dropped, both before and after the show opens.

Original orchestrations of most early musicals have been lost because no one thought that future generations would want them. Published sheet music of older songs was often quite different from the version that was done onstage. To reach a broad market of musical amateurs, publishers often chose a "sheet-music key" so that the highest note of a song would be on the top line or space of the treble clef, regardless of how the song was sung in the show. They would also double every melody note in the piano part, even though this often does not result in a good sound. Sheet-music keys were usually used in books of "selections" from musicals.

If you want to audition for a musical, it may be important to find out exactly what vocal range is needed for the part you want to play. This information is found in the complete published score of a musical. Correct keys are also used in books of selections from more recent musicals.

**"It Don't Mean a Thing,"** page 220. Edward Kennedy "Duke" Ellington (Washington, D.C., 1899–New York, 1974) composed over 6,000 works, but he also performed continuously and had the organizational skill to lead a major band for decades.

**"Love Is Here to Stay,"** page 224. When George Gershwin (Brooklyn, 1898–Hollywood, 1937) died, he was working on songs for a film, *The Goldwyn Follies* (1938). Normally words are written before music, but in this case Gershwin wrote the melody without having any words in mind for it. His brother Ira added these words later. Kenny Baker sang the song in the film.

**"Over the Rainbow,"** page 232. Harold Arlen's songs for *The Wizard of Oz* are early and outstanding examples of movie songs that were integral to the character and plot development of the film. The sheet music that is still published includes a verse that is not sung in the film, and it is in E♭. Judy Garland sang the song a fifth lower, in A♭. She also treated the rhythm freely, and it is worthwhile to study her performance. One consistent change: she begins the third measure of the chorus with a quarter-note rest and sings "way" as a quarter note. All similar measures are sung the same way.

**"I'll Know,"** page 235, from *Guys and Dolls* (1950, 1,200 performances). Based on stories by Damon Runyon, this show portrays a battle of wits between New York gangsters and Salvation Army officers. This song is sung by one of the latter, Miss Sarah Brown (Isabel Bigley on stage, and Jean Simmons in the film).

**"They Say It's Wonderful,"** page 238. Irving Berlin wrote about 1,500 published songs, although he could not read music and played the piano only in F♯. *Annie Get Your Gun* (1946, 1,147 performances on its first Broadway run) starred Ethel Merman, whose name was synonymous with belt singing. It told the story of Annie Oakley, a sharpshooter and circus performer.

**"A Cockeyed Optimist,"** page 242, from *South Pacific* (1949, 1,925 performances), occurs in the first scene, when Ensign Nellie Forbush, a U.S. Navy nurse in World War II, expresses her philosophy of life to a handsome French civilian. Mary Martin created the role of Nellie, who seemed to have a flair for unusual verbal images: "When the sky is a bright canary yellow"; "But every whippoorwill is selling me a bill" (a play on "sold a bill of goods"); "life is just a bowl of jello" (a play on "life is just a bowl of cherries"). The musical is based on James Michener's *Tales of the South Pacific*. Original key: F.

**"One Hand, One Heart,"** page 246, from *West Side Story* (1957, 732 performances). A great conductor and composer of classical music, Leonard Bernstein (1918–1990) wrote the music for this modern version of the Romeo and Juliet story. These wedding vows are sung by the young lovers, Maria (Carol Lawrence) and Tony (Larry Kert), in a bridal shop after closing time. Original key: G♭.

**"Soon It's Gonna Rain,"** page 250, from *The Fantasticks* (1960, over 16,900 performances and still running as this is written). Fans who saw this show on a date now bring their grandchildren to see it in the same tiny theater in Greenwich Village. This song is a duet between the young lovers, Luisa and Matt. Original key: C.

**"Make Someone Happy,"** page 255, from *Do Re Mi* (1960, 400 performances). The show is a satire on the music business and the way hit songs are created. This hit was first sung by John Reardon. Original key: E♭.

**"In My Life,"** page 258. John Lennon and Paul McCartney put their names jointly on all of the Beatles' songs, but this song is thought to be mostly Lennon's. Although it is not their most famous, "In My Life" is much admired by other song writers.

**"Happiness,"** page 260, from *You're a Good Man, Charlie Brown* (1967, 1,597 performances). Based on the *Peanuts* comic strip, this show was released as a record before it was staged.

**"Once Upon a Dream,"** page 263, is sung twice in *Jekyll and Hyde.* In the famous horror story written by Robert Louis Stevenson, the idealistic Dr. Jekyll experiments with drugs that he thinks will aid humanity. The drugs turn him instead into a murderous psychopath who goes by the name of Mr. Hyde. Lisa, the woman whom Dr. Jekyll loves, sees that she is losing him and sings this song of regret, performed in E major with the text printed here. Later, Jekyll sings the same melody in G major, with even more despairing words. The voice part is not doubled in the original orchestration, and mm. 34 and 35 have no accompaniment.

**"Believe in Yourself,"** page 266, from *The Wiz* (1975, 1,672 performances). Based on L. Frank Baum's *The Wizard of Oz*, this musical had an entirely African American cast. In the final scene of the successful film, Dorothy, played by Diana Ross, sings this song to Scarecrow, Tin Woodman, and Lion. The whole song is sung again, with some altered words, by Glenda the Good, sung by Lena Horne. Both stars sing the song in B♭ major, beginning on F below middle C. The sheet music key is a fifth higher.

**"What I Did for Love,"** page 270, from *A Chorus Line* (1975, 6,137 performances) is sung by Diana Morales, who is auditioning to be in the chorus of a musical. When a dancer injures himself, perhaps ending his career, the director asks the other auditioners how they would feel if their careers ended suddenly. Morales (first sung by Priscilla Lopez) answers with this song about her love of dancing. Original key: A♭.

**"In a Simple Way I Love You,"** page 274, from *I'm Getting My Act Together and Taking It on the Road*. Gretchen Cryer played the role of a performer who is struggling with the end of a relationship and the preparations for a concert tour. This song embodies the past for her.

**"Loving You,"** page 277, is from *Passion*, which takes place at an army post in Italy in the 1800s. A depressed and obsessive woman falls in love with a captain who tries to be kind but does not return her love. Donna Murphy sang the role of Fosca (the Italian word means "dark, gloomy"). Stephen Sondheim is the finest dramatist in musical theater today, although not all of his scores are popular successes. This song is a major third lower in the score.

**"Whistle Down the Wind,"** page 280, from the musical of the same name. The scene is in the southern United States (although the musical opened in London). In this song a father and children are consoling themselves for the death of their wife and mother by singing her favorite song. The first words mean to whistle loudly enough, assert one's self enough, to be heard in spite of adverse situations. Original key: D.

# The International Phonetic Alphabet

**Sounds of English**

These are the symbols of the International Phonetic Alphabet (IPA) as they are used in singing English. They are given in this order: vowels, semivowels, consonants. You can learn more about their use in Chapters 6 and 7 and about diphthongs in Chapter 8.

**Vowels:**

| | | | |
|---|---|---|---|
| 1. | [i] | Ee | we, meet, key, sea, receive |
| 2. | [ɪ] | Short I | with, gym, lily, listen |
| 3. | [e] | Pure Ay | chaotic, dictates |
| 4. | [ɛ] | Open Eh | enter, merry, many, friend |
| 5. | [æ] | Short A | at, stab, act, shadow, magic |
| 6. | [a] | Bright Ah | aisle (substitute #5 or #7) |
| 7. | [ɑ] | Dark Ah | far, dark, calm, palm (silent l) |
| 8. | [ɒ] | Short O | god, long (substitute #7) |
| 9. | [ɔ] | Open O | chord, author, awe, shawl |
| 10. | [o] | Pure Oh | hotel, obey |
| 11. | [ʊ] | Short U | bush, foot, wolf, look |
| 12. | [u] | Oo | flute, queue, noon, do, you |
| 13. | [ʌ] | Uh | sung, up, son, come |
| 14. | [ə] | Schwa | (second syllable of:) even, sofa, little |
| 15. | [ɜ] | Er | learn, her, bird, journey, myrrh |

**Semivowels:**

| | | | |
|---|---|---|---|
| 16. | [j] | Yah | yam, union, eulogy, pew, due |
| 17. | [w] | Wah | was, witch, waste, once |

**Consonants:**

| | | | |
|---|---|---|---|
| 18. | [m] | Em | sum, ma'am, dimmer, hymn |
| 19. | [n] | En | nun, liner |
| 20. | [ŋ] | Ing | sang, king, hunger, English |
| 21. | [l] | El | love, wilt, Sally |
| 22. | [r] | Ahr | red, earring, hear |
| 23. | [h] | Aitch | house, hunk, Minnehaha |
| 24. | [hw] | Which | why, whether, whiz |
| 25. | [f] | Eff | far, feel, philosophy |
| 26. | [v] | Vee | very, overt, quiver |
| 27. | [θ] | Theta | thick, thistle, cloth |
| 28. | [ð] | Edh | these, other, within, lathe |
| 29. | [s] | Ess | sat, psalm, lets, decent |
| 30. | [z] | Zee | zoom, buzzard, was, zest |
| 31. | [ʃ] | Shah | shoe, negotiate, sugar, cash |
| 32. | [ʒ] | Zsa-Zsa | leisure, garage, casual |
| 33. | [p] | Pee | pay, caper, sup |
| 34. | [b] | Bee | boy, saber, rub |
| 35. | [t] | Tee | tent, ptomaine, slat |

| 36. | [d] | Dee | die, leader, bed |
| 37. | [k] | Kay | coal, choir, technique, anchor |
| 38. | [g] | Hard Gee | girl, bigger, bug |
| 39. | [ʧ] | Cha-Cha | cello, rich, catcher |
| 40. | [ʤ] | Soft Gee | jet, jasmine, ajar, huge |

**Diphthongs:**

| 4 + 2. | [ɛɪ] | Long Ay | wave, wait, weigh, way |
| 6 + 2. | [aɪ] | Long I | life, pie, cry, aisle, Einstein |
| 9 + 2. | [ɔɪ] | Oy | boy, choice |
| 6 + 11. | [aʊ] | Ow | wow, ouch |
| 10 + 11. | [oʊ] | Long Oh | social, sew, blow, groan |
| 2 + 14. | [ɪɚ] | Ear-Diphthong | cheer, fear, mere, we're |
| 4 + 14. | [ɛɚ] | Air-Diphthong | care, hair, wear, they're |
| 6 + 14. | [aɚ] | Are-Diphthong | car, hearth, armor |
| 9 + 14. | [ɔɚ] | Or-Diphthong | lord, pour, your, o'er |
| 11 + 14. | [ʊɚ] | Tour-Diphthong | sure, moor, your |
| 6 + 2 + 14. | [aɪɚ] | Ire-Triphthong | fire, briar, lyre, choir |
| 6 + 11 + 14. | [aʊɚ] | Our-Triphthong | cower, sour |

# Sounds of Other Languages

English equivalents for these sounds do not exist. They are listed by alphabetical order as the symbols resemble letters.

Notice that in all non-English languages the symbol [r] stands for Rolled R, never American R.

| [ː] | Lengthener | Hold the position of the previous vowel or consonant. (Ge, It, Sw) |
| [ã] | Nasal Ah | Vowel resonated in both mouth and nose. (Fr) |
| [β] | Buzz | Voiced vibration of both lips. (Sp) |
| [ç] | Ich sound | Voiceless fricative, like strong [h] in "huge." (Ge) |
| [ɛ̃] | Nasal Open Eh | Vowel resonated in both mouth and nose. (Fr) |
| [ʝ] | Curly J | Voiced fricative consonant, with the tongue tip down, using friction of air between the tongue hump and hard palate. (Ge, Sp) |
| [ʎ] | Elya | Like [lj] in "million," but with the tongue tip down. (It, Sp) |
| [ɲ] | Enya | Like [nj] in "onion," but with the tongue tip down. (Fr, It, Sp) |
| [õ] | Nasal Pure Oh | Vowel resonated in both mouth and nose. (Fr) |
| [œ] | O-E | [ɛ] with rounded lips. (Fr, Ge, Sw) |
| [œ̃] | Nasal O-E | [œ] with rounded lips. (Fr) |
| [ø] | Ay-Oh | [e] with rounded lips. (Fr, Ge, Sw) |
| [ɵ] | Barred O | Vowel between [ø] and [o]. (Sw) |
| [ɾ] | Flipped R | Single tongue tap, as in British "very." (Fr, It, Sp) |
| [ʉ] | Barred U | Vowel between [y] and [u]. (Sw) |
| [ɣ] | Agua | Voiced form of [x]. (Sp) |
| [x] | Ach sound | Voiceless friction of air between the back of the tongue and the soft palate. (Ge, He, Sp) |
| [y] | Ee-Oo | [i] with rounded lips. (Fr, Ge, Sw) |
| [ʏ] | Short I-U | [ɪ] with rounded lips. (Ge) |

# Index of Persons and Song Sources

# Index of Vocal and Musical Terms